BUILDING A CITY

100 Years of Melbourne Architecture

Granville Wilson and Peter Sands

Melbourne
Oxford University Press
Oxford Auckland New York

Oxford University Press

OXFORD LONDON GLASGOW
NEW YORK TORONTO MELBOURNE AUCKLAND
KUALA LUMPUR SINGAPORE HONG KONG TOKYO
DELHI BOMBAY CALCUTTA MADRAS KARACHI
NAIROBI DAR ES SALAAM CAPE TOWN

© *Granville Wilson and Peter Sands 1981*

First published 1981

NATIONAL LIBRARY OF AUSTRALIA CATALOGUING IN
PUBLICATION DATA

Wilson, Granville, 1922-
  Building a city.

  Bibliography
  Includes index
  ISBN 0 19 554292 4

  1. Architecture — Melbourne — History.
  2. Historic buildings — Melbourne. I.
  3. Sands, Peter, 1946-. I. Title.

720'.9945'1

DESIGNED BY GUY MIRABELLA
TYPESET BY COMPSET PRODUCTION COMPANY LIMITED
PRINTED IN HONG KONG BY BRIGHT SUN PRINTING PRESS CO., LTD.
PUBLISHED BY OXFORD UNIVERSITY PRESS, 7 BOWEN CRESCENT, MELBOURNE

Contents

This book is intended as a guide to the first one hundred years of Melbourne architecture for the increasing number of people who are interested in the fine old buildings around the city and suburbs.

These buildings record different periods in Melbourne's history: the primitive wattle and daub cottages built by the early settlers out of the crude natural resources; the mid-Victorian residential and public buildings that succeeded them, monuments to the superb trade skills of craftsmen attracted to Victoria by the Gold Rush; the grand mansions of the Boom Era, redolent with the opulence and confidence of their owners; the great Gothic Revival churches and cathedrals; the riot of the late nineteenth-century Victoriana; the many extravagant and eclectic examples of Queen Anne and Edwardian architecture; and the modern work of the 1930s that is now the focus of renewed interest.

Already far too many fine old buildings around Melbourne have been demolished in the name of progress and replaced by new buildings quite out of harmony with the identity of the area in which they are set. Even as this introduction is being written, the A.P.A. Building in Elizabeth Street is being torn down, while voracious bulldozers threaten some of the lovely Victorian terraces in Royal Parade. This surely would not be allowed to happen if more people were aware of the historical, architectural and aesthetic value of buildings such as these.

We hope that this book, which arose out of our shared interest in the subject, will

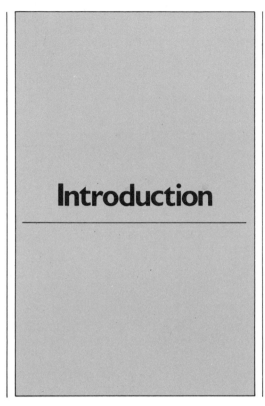

Introduction

place Melbourne buildings in their historical and architectural context and will contribute towards an increased appreciation of our city's unique architectural heritage.

Acknowledgements

We gratefully acknowledge help in research from the following people: Miss Elison Harvie, Miss Mary Turner Shaw, Mrs Rosalind Landells, Mr Wilson Evans, Mr Peter Leadbeater, Mr Gordon Rushman, Mr Edward Fielder Billson, Mr John Edwards, Mr Bill Thomas, Mr Peter Staughton, Mr Neil Clerehan, Mr Randall Heinrich, Ms Judith Trimble, Mr Robert Vincent, the late Mr Leslie Grant, Mrs Helen Newcombe for typing, and Mr Neil Rooney of the National Trust.

We should like to thank Ms Jenepher Duncan of the Department of Visual Arts at Monash University for the photograph of Eastbourne House, Mr Adrian Featherson for that of Bendigo Hotel and Mr M. Bernardi for that of the now demolished building, 45 Spring Street. We are grateful to Mr Mark Strizic for kind permission to publish his photographs of Tara, and to Mr Peter Hill for photographic assistance.

Especial thanks are due to Dr Miles Lewis of the University of Melbourne, Mrs Mary Lewis of the State Library of Victoria and Mrs B.J. Savill of the Royal Historical Society of Victoria; and to all the people who have generously made available private homes for study and photography.

Ilford (Australia) Pty Ltd have generously supported photographic work in this book by providing materials and technical assistance.

In 1835 Alexis de Tocqueville called America *une feuille blanche*, a blank page, upon which history waited to be written. At that time the same could have been said of Melbourne; but years before Port Phillip Bay was discovered, before there was even a blank page to be worked on, there was a shadowy movement of very lonely ships on the southern ocean. Tasman, Cook, Bass and Flinders stand out as fearless explorers and well could they echo Coleridge's lines, 'We were the first that ever burst into that silent sea'.

To James Cook and Joseph Banks, New Holland was a great unknown continent and when the nineteenth century began the southern coastline was still uncharted. It was the French threat at sea presenting a rival claim to an empire-building nation which spurred the British to chart the whole coastline.

James Grant entered Western Port in the *Lady Nelson* in 1801 and John Murray sailed up Port Phillip Bay the following year, taking possession in the name of King George III.[1] Matthew Flinders, during his circumnavigation of the continent, followed in the *Investigator*, climbing Arthur's Seat and surveying the bay from the top of the You Yangs.[2]

In 1803 Charles Grimes was sent by Governor King to make a survey of Port Phillip Bay. The aim of this expedition was twofold: to thwart any French imperial ambitions and to find the most favourable place for a settlement. Together with Charles Robbins and James Fleming, he explored the Saltwater (now Maribyrnong)

Chapter 1

Explorers and Pioneers

For them no more the blazing hearth shall burn/Or busy housewife ply her evening care.
Thomas Gray, *Elegy written in a country churchyard*

River and the Yarra, continuing up the latter as far as Dight's Falls. He recommended the banks of the Yarra as the ideal place for a settlement. It is worthwhile noting that this pre-dated John Batman's 'discovery' by thirty-two years.

Two months after Grimes left Port Phillip, David Collins' expedition arrived from London, in two ships carrying marines, convicts and free settlers. Ironically, Collins was unaware of the favourable report by Grimes. The site of his abortive attempt at settlement at Sullivan Bay near Sorrento can still be seen. To Collins the bay was uninviting and not conducive to permanent settlement. He withdrew to the Derwent which was known and settled.[3] William Buckley escaped from this expedition, adopted the Aborigines' way of life and was lost to civilization for thirty years. During those years the bay was silent.

Excepting a call for wood or water by passing vessels and occasional visits by sealers and whalers, Europeans left the Port Phillip blacks and their white friend Buckley in peace.[4]

During this time there were incredible exploits by overlanders. In 1824 Hamilton Hume and William Hovell journeyed from New South Wales across the Murray, thence to Corio Bay and back.

A second attempt to establish a settlement took place at Settlement Point (Corinella) on the shores of Western Port in 1826, under the command of Captain Wright, but it was officially abandoned two years later. However Strzelecki arrived there in 1840 and was hospitably received by convicts who had found refuge there.

Portland was settled by the Hentys in 1834 and Victoria was opened up to pastoralists from New South Wales and Van Diemen's Land in the wake of Thomas Mitchell, who explored the country in 1836 from north-east to south-west, giving the name 'Australia Felix' to an area of Victoria which included a huge volcanic plain now known as the Western District. Jumping ahead chronologically, it was this area, favoured by a rich soil, a warm climate and a plentiful water supply, which was seen by squatters for its potential firstly for sheep and later for cattle and crops. Among the first was Dr A. Thompson, who landed sheep at Point Henry in 1836. There followed a steady invasion of Scottish Lowlanders, educated at Oxford or Cambridge and Presbyterian by conviction, who left their cultural stamp on this area and for the most part had an anchorage in Melbourne in the form of a town house.

The founding of Melbourne had to await the arrival of a group of adventurers from Van Diemen's Land in 1835. John Batman's party arrived on the *Rebecca* and John Pascoe Fawkner's on the *Enterprise*. Batman's primary concern was for sheep pasturage and this was the motive behind his famous land deal with the natives which the British Government later declined to ratify. On the banks of the Yarra somewhere near the present Queen's Bridge he noted in his diary, 'This will be the place for a village'.[5] Fawkner also landed and began to build and plant. Whilst Batman died young, Fawkner founded the town's first newspapers and lived till 1869.

Batman's vision, as noted, had been for sheep pasturage, and there followed a steady stream of immigrants from Van Diemen's Land, guided in by a barrel mounted on a staff on Point Gellibrand. (This was later replaced by an oil lamp on a wooden lattice tower.) Ships could run in on the sand where Commonwealth Reserve in Williamstown is now. Thousands of sheep

were unloaded here, ate their way inland and founded Victoria's wool industry. (Geelong and Portland, of course, were also entry points for pastoralists and sheep.)

At this point ships could ride at anchor or proceed to Sandridge (Port Melbourne) where Wilbraham Liardet settled in 1839. From there a series of markers through the bush would direct travellers to the 'Settlement', or 'Bearbrass', as Melbourne was first called. Alternatively, ships could proceed up the tortuous course of the Yarra as far as the Falls (Queen's Bridge).

Geologically speaking, Melbourne was built, though not all at once, on four hills: Batman's Hill, since levelled for Spencer Street Railway Station, Emerald Hill (South Melbourne), the hill now occupied by Government House, and the rising ground in the Fitzroy area. On 10 June 1836 George Stewart, the police magistrate from Goulburn, reported that

> the town, Bearbrass, is on the left hand of the Yarro Yarro, about seven miles from its mouth, which at present consists of thirteen buildings, viz, three weatherboard, two slab, and eight turf huts.[6]

There were also twelve or fifteen tents, a population of 127 people and 26 500 sheep.

Arriving in February 1840, Jonathan

Plan showing the allotments for the first land sale in Melbourne in 1837. This was the beginning of the land boom which lasted till the first depression in 1842. Note the little streets providing rear access to the lots, and the allocation of blocks reserved for church (St James's), marketplace and customs (nearest the water)

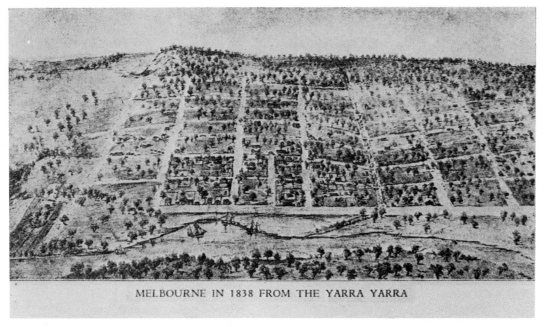
MELBOURNE IN 1838 FROM THE YARRA YARRA

Binns Were found 'good shops with Drugs, Groceries, Haberdashery, Ironmongery; indeed each shop seemed to be quite an Emporium'. He also found many young well-dressed squatters. Compared with the hardships of Port Jackson, the new settlement had everything going for it. Writing home, Robert Russell commented:

The soil in this country is superior to any in the colony, we have a good grazing land, and a fine supply of water; a fine harbour, a Town on which much capital (I am afraid to say how much) has been expended, enterprising settlers and flocks and herds in-creasing in all directions, a climate well fitted for Englishmen, and events hastening forward the necessity for some scheme of extended emigration from which we shall soon feel the benefit.[7]

There are many descriptions of the Yarra as teeming with fish, swan, duck and teal, but in reality it was a dangerously polluted river at an early stage, and settlers, after enduring the rigours of an ocean voyage, were succumbing to disease. Georgiana McCrae noted in her journal of 1842 that 'infantile cholera and dysentery are just now decimating the children'.

The Yarra was depended upon for communication, water supply and drainage. Thomas Watt was the first man to operate a punt across the river, but lost his licence through enticing workers from the nearby brickfields with free liquor. John Walsh took over by operating a punt on the present site of Prince's Bridge. When Alexander Sim began work on the new St James's Cathedral he operated two punts across the river. In 1840 Charles Henry Le Souef inaugurated a ferry service about ten yards above the Falls, which were where the present Queen's Bridge spans the river. The water above this was fresh and constituted the town's only water supply. But this water was brackish at high tide. An attempt to overcome this problem was a dam across the Falls, constructed of stone, mud and mortar by a convict road gang in 1839. It was 'simple, neat, and substantial' (*Port Phillip Gazette*) but by 1841 it was in ruins.

Later, water was pumped from above Prince's Bridge and distributed by water cart; but wool-scouring and other industries polluted this supply. James Blackburn, who came to Melbourne as a ticket-of-leave man in 1849, formed the Melbourne Water Company and became Town Surveyor. After experimenting with the Yarra water with pumps and filters, he devised a scheme for tapping the Plenty River at Yan Yean and conveying water to Melbourne by pipe and aqueduct. Yan Yean water reached Melbourne in 1857, but Blackburn had died of typhoid fever in 1854.

Burial Hill (Flagstaff Gardens) commemorates the first deaths in the settlement.

A drawing of Melbourne town in 1838 showing the grid pattern of streets aligned on the Yarra bank at the point where the ships could pull in.
Topographical features like Flagstaff Gardens and the creek bed along what is now Elizabeth Street can be appreciated

3

(Melbourne's later burial ground became the site of the Victoria Market.) On Burial Hill a good view could be had of the shipping, so a flagstaff was erected to signal the arrival of ships in the bay.

In 1837, the year of Queen Victoria's accession to the throne, Governor Richard Bourke arrived in March to inspect the town and surrounding district. He named the town Melbourne after Queen Victoria's first Prime Minister and the streets after prominent persons of the day. With this official party came Robert Hoddle, whose work as a surveyor did much to shape Melbourne's street patterns (see Chapter 8).

The first land sales in the present city area were held on 1 June 1837; the minimum price for an allotment was £5 ($10). The purchaser was to erect within a year a house to the value of £50 ($100) and he was not permitted to make any carriageways across the footpaths, as access had been provided from Hoddle's back street or mews. John Batman built a two-storey brick house on the south-west corner of William and Collins Streets.

The town of Melbourne was now official. Government and administrative positions were filled during 1837, and 140 ships arrived, bringing 740 immigrants. At the second land sale the highest price, £100 ($200), was paid by John Batman for the allotment on the north-west corner of Flinders and Swanston Streets.

The early citizens lived a full, if rough, life. The first races were held on a course from Batman's Hill to the site of the North Melbourne Railway Station. There was a town band, and healthy sport was encouraged to combat drunkenness. Before 1838 was out the Melbourne Club had been founded and a cricket match played between the military and the civilians. And so 'in countless ways the citizens of Melbourne were unconsciously countering the loneliness of a small community in a strange land by re-creating the familiar'.[8] It was a transplanted society disciplined by the tyranny of distance. Bound by the various assumptions they had acquired by upbringing, community leaders strove to re-create the society of Regency and early Victorian England, with its customs and standards, its romanticism, its radical politics and its evangelical faith.

Land prices rose towards the end of the 1930s. C.H. Ebden sold for £10 250 ($20 500) three blocks in Collins Street which originally cost him £54 ($108). The population doubled in 1840-41. Champagne luncheons accompanied land selling to such an extent that it was said that the whole country for miles around Melbourne was strewn with champagne bottles. This was not to last.

Samuel Jackson, Melbourne's first architect, who had come over from Launceston in Fawkner's party, has left us a sketch of the early town which can be seen in the State Library. He drew it from the half-finished walls of the first Scots Church, which he designed. Garryowen described the town:

Melbourne in 1840 was certainly not a city and could hardly be called a town; nor did it even partake of the characteristics of a village or hamlet. It was a kind of big 'settlement', in groups pitched here and there, with houses, sheds, and tents in clusters, or scattered in ones or twos. There were streets marked out, and stores, shops, and counting-houses; but, with the exception of those in the old market square and portions of Flinders, Little Flinders, Collins and Elizabeth Streets, so dispersed that, after dark, residents incurred not only trouble but danger in moving about. The taverns, or houses of entertainment, were few in number, and, with a couple of exceptions, the accommodation for the public was of the most limited and comfortless description. There were several brick-built houses and a few weatherboard cottages, with some, though not much, pretension to comfort; but the majority of the business or residential tenements were made up of colonial wattle-and-daub, roofed with sheets of bark or coarse shingle, for slates or tiles were not to be thought of, and the corrugated iron age had not arrived.[9]

The area known as 'Government Block' was bounded by Collins, King, Bourke and Spencer Streets. Here stood Captain Lonsdale's first cottage and tents were erected here for Bourke's visit. The block is significant for the erection of Melbourne's first public buildings: a brick and weatherboard hospital for convicts; prisoners' barracks;

wattle-and-plaster military huts and an officers' servants' room. The gaol on this block was burnt down and was replaced in 1841 by a new gaol described in Chapter 3. In 1840 Robert Hoddle purchased the south-eastern corner of Bourke and Spencer Streets for his home.

Land in Flinders Street, where John Pascoe Fawkner's twelve-roomed house was sited, was set aside as 'Customs Reserve' and Fawkner's house was demolished to make way for the Customs House. Mr Young, colonial architect, prepared plans and John Jones Peers, who founded the Master Builders' Association in 1839, tendered successfully. However by 1840 rising prices demanded the calling of fresh tenders and Patrick Main continued the structure. This two-storey building, which was described as ugly, is not the building we see today on the site.

Around Melbourne the pioneers were settling and building, and today we often forget the privations they suffered. The early records tell of one family losing two children in the first six days of the voyage out and another a few days later.[10] When the cottages were built the pangs of homesickness would be softened by the sight of a candle in another cottage window. So where settlement took place there was a strong 'togetherness', for the bush was still thick and people were getting lost in it between Melbourne and Richmond. Richmond was beautiful with its red gums. George Gordon McCrae commented: 'Amongst the trees the weatherboard cottages of the settlers looked very pretty'.[11]

At this stage a brief survey of the greater Melbourne area will give us a better picture of the pattern of development. The development has been markedly lopsided, its growth, or sprawl, being in an easterly direction. There are many reasons for this: geologically, the north and west have shallower soils than the east and basalt not far below the surface, which increases the cost of foundations and services. Climatically, the area to the north and west has a lower rainfall; and aesthetically, much of it is flat, treeless and windswept, whereas the east is undulating, wooded, better watered and closer to the Dandenongs.

We shall start with Brighton on the bayside and pan round in an anti-clockwise direction, necessitating in the process some jumps in chronology.

The only road south (later the Nepean Highway) led across the sand belt to Arthur's Seat and to the historically rich area around Portsea and Sorrento, where the she-oaks were sacrificed to burn lime. Astride this road and 5 miles (8 kilometres) from Melbourne, Henry Dendy selected his 'special survey' in 1841, thus acquiring virtually the town of Brighton.[12] Along the coast were planned large marine villa blocks, while inland along the watercourse (later Elwood Canal) the village area of Little Brighton grew. A number of immigrants of the trade and labouring classes, among them the Lindsay brothers, bricklayers, arrived with Dendy, found work on the estate and built timber and bark cottages.[13] Early cottages in Brighton, such as Merrow in St Kilda Street and Snook's Cottage in New

Street, were constructed with these Lindsay bricks which are now rendered over because of their porosity.

The eastern suburbs were thick with messmate, peppermint, stringybark, wattle and box, and timber-cutting and providing transport to the Fitzroy market were the earliest occupations; but the lines of communication were strained to the limit. Starting from the inner suburbs and moving out, the growing popularity of Emerald Hill (South Melbourne), St Kilda and Brighton brought settlers south-east by St Kilda Road. The great estates of Como, Grey Lodge and Toorak House comprised most of Toorak. Between the grounds of Toorak House and St Kilda there was 'trackless forest'.[14]

Further afield John Gardiner's cattle run covered most of Malvern until the first Crown land sales of 1854. There were two more special surveys east of the Yarra—that of Elgar in the Camberwell–Balwyn area and that of Unwin further out up Koonung Creek.

The White Horse Hotel flourished in Box Hill while Cobb and Co. serviced the vineyards further east and the Yarra valley goldfields during the fifties. This continued until the railway network competed with coach travel later in the century and finally won. In Doncaster, where the higher ground was densely timbered and hard to work, the settlement of the district had been along the river flats until in 1853 German pioneers formed a settlement called Waldau ('clearing in the forest').

The Yarra valley has strongly influenced

5

the growth of Melbourne, channelling development up its course and retarding it to the south-east due to the lack of bridges. In 1836 Gardiner, Hawdon and Hepburn brought 300 head of cattle from New South Wales, grazed them in the area of Yarra Bend National Park and crossed the river at Dight's Falls. Whereas the early settlers had preferred the country to the north and west of Melbourne for sheep, in the fifties the country to the south and east was taken up for gardening and fruit-growing. Thus Boroondara (Kew–Hawthorn) opened up and the Yarra was crossed in several places, first by punt and then by bridge.

Choice sites overlooking the Yarra were taken up for homesteads, and 6 miles (10 kilometres) up the valley from Melbourne Warringal (Heidelberg) was founded, where Hawdon the overlander built Banyule in 1846 on a ridge overlooking the Yarra valley. Further upstream Warrandyte was found to be ideal for cattle; and Yerring had just the right climate for vines. The Yarra and its tributaries, Plenty River and Diamond Creek, were peaceful until the discovery of gold, which gave rise to further little settlements like Panton Hill and St Andrews.

In the north the lines of communication were extended by George Evans, who in 1836 followed Deep Creek up to Sunbury and built Emu Bottom. William Jackson proceeded twenty miles up the Saltwater River, and, acting for John Pascoe Fawkner, took possession of a large tract of land running east from the river, comprising portions of Keilor, Glenroy, Pascoe Vale and Coburg. The bush track north from Melbourne crossed Merri Creek where Joseph Pentridge, an Irish immigrant, bought a few acres of land on which the present gaol stands.

The creek cut its way through the basalt plain and exposed large faces of bluestone, which was used to pave the road (later Sydney Road or Hume Highway). Convicts employed in this work were housed in a temporary stockade where, according to Father Patrick Dunne, the prisoners were 'stowed away like swine to sleep on wooden benches'.[15]

East of this the land between Merri and Darebin Creeks was opened up to auction in 1839 and cleared for isolated farms and industries. In 1864 the first reservoir was constructed, fed by an aqueduct from the Yan Yean basin and giving its name (Reservoir) to the area.

German Lutherans arrived in 1849 and 1850 and a square mile (2.6 square kilometres) was made available to them about twelve miles (19 kilometres) north of Melbourne. Land was bought at £1 an acre ($2 for less than half a hectare) and buildings were erected using the local bluestone. This was known as Westgarthtown, now part of Lalor.

Expansion westwards was limited by the West Melbourne Swamp, which covered most of the area below Spencer Street west to the Maribyrnong River on the edge of Footscray. Not only was this swamp fed by Moonie Ponds Creek but by most of the drainage from the main township, including sewage which often ran in open drains. This condition and the course of the Maribyrnong, which has been as formative as the Yarra in the development of Melbourne, tended to isolate the Williamstown community.

Williamstown, named after William IV, was the place for government stores, shipping facilities and control of the port waters. Its development was restricted through the shortage of water, ground water being obtained from the Kororoit Creek area west of the town. It was a small community and 'almost the entire population earned its living in some way upon the waters of Hobson's Bay. Many residents spent their time in bay and river fishing. Houses were small and crudely built, the people poor, and money for amenities almost non-existent'.[16]

Williamstown was linked to Sandridge (Port Melbourne) by steam ferry, but some travellers preferred to walk or ride to Melbourne using the punt across the Saltwater River at the foot of the present Bunbury Street, Footscray, and following the track round the present Yarraville Gardens. Along this route Superintendent La Trobe planned several 'villages' or stages to link Melbourne and Williamstown, but these have not survived. The road was a summer one, the black soil making it impassable for anything heavier than a horse and rider in wet weather.

From Williamstown was supplied bluestone in quantity alike for construction work and for outward-bound sailing ships light in ballast. After the failure of the gold mines many a hard rock man found work here. A vast basalt plain stretched away to the Chirnsides' great property on the Werribee River, to the You Yangs and on into the Western District.

Port Melbourne was made more accessible to Melbourne by means of the construction of City Road, using immigrant labour as a relief measure during the depression of 1842, and the first railway in Victoria connected the two places in 1857. Port Melbourne was the voyager's landfall and virtually Melbourne's front door. So also was Spencer Street Station until the opening of the airports at Essendon and Tullamarine in this century.

Its history changed dramatically with the cutting of a canal to eliminate the sharp curve of Fishermen's Bend, a scheme proposed by Sir John Coode. This was to shorten the tortuous river passage by more than a mile (2 kilometres). He further proposed the dredging of the channel to 25 feet (7.6 metres) and the formation of a series of docks. The Coode Canal was opened in 1886 and the course of the Yarra was shortened to a gentle curve. With the filling of Lorimer Street and the deposit of dredged material the vast swamplands of Sandridge Flats gradually became useful and the ground was prepared for Garden City (see Chapter 8).

Having noted the pattern of development of greater Melbourne and the movement of its early settlers, we shall now look at its resources and its architecture.

Thirty-four years before Melbourne was founded James Grant built a log blockhouse 24 feet by 12 feet (7.3 × 3.6 metres) on Churchill Island. It was built of tree trunks held in position by supporting verticals, suggesting an early example of horizontal slab construction. The use of slabs, either sawn or split, became common practice in Victoria, especially where good splitting timber like ironbark and stringybark was plentiful, and is still to be seen in isolated farming areas. Robert Russell noted: 'They can get slabs (that is split trees which are inserted in a groove at top and bottom and driven tight) and thus a strong building is formed without need of nails and it can be thatched or covered with bark and be plastered so as to render it quite water-tight'.[1]

A variation was described by Georgiana McCrae in her diary of 1845: 'Our house is built of gum tree slabs supported, horizontally, by grooved corner posts, and the same artiface (used again) for windows and doors'.

The gaps between split slabs were filled with mud, plaster or strips of timber. Generally, vertical slabs were used for sheds and outhouses and horizontal slabs for more important structures. A noteworthy example of slab construction is Gulf Station near Yarra Glen, a homestead of the early 1850s, where the timber has mellowed to a soft grey. This method of construction was more popular on the goldfields than in Melbourne.

In Melbourne itself the first buildings were less permanent. A sod hut had been

Chapter 2

Early Melbourne Architecture

There is no such thing as primitive man, merely primitive resources.
Le Corbusier

built for John Batman's party at Indented Head and also for Henry Batman on the south-east corner of William and Collins Streets. This was traditional construction in parts of Europe and Ireland, and settlers of the peasant class would have been familiar with it. In the early years there were many sod buildings in the Melbourne area and in the country around Port Fairy. As a building material it was damp and impermanent.

Sometimes the bark from box, blackbutt and stringybark was used for wall and roof cladding. It was fastened to the framework with strips of hide and held down with poles laid horizontally. Because of its obvious fire hazard and its capacity for shrinkage it was considered a temporary material. It was much used in Gippsland where giant eucalypts were plentiful.

Another roofing material was thatch. In Melbourne the long reed from the Yarra

Gulf Station, Yarra Glen (1850s). An early example of a homestead built of slab construction with rough-hewn local box. The whole complex of buildings, which once housed a whole community, is in harmony with its surroundings

was used and, throughout the Western District, ripe straw or tall tussock grass. Owing to its fire risk thatch gave way to hardwood shingles and later to iron and slate. Sod was sometimes used on roofs but its weight on unbraced timber structures was often excessive. It can still be seen over farm shelters in country areas.

Wattle and daub was a method of construction traditional throughout Europe under many different names. Those who

An early example (date unknown) of sod and thatch roofing on a farm shelter at Parwan, near Bacchus Marsh, indicating a sort of unconscious local language in building. There are other examples in the Eppalock area

wish to go further into these early building methods are referred to *Victorian Primitive* by Miles Lewis,[3] who traces them back to European antecedents.

In the greater Melbourne area and in the country, variations of wattle and daub or half-timbered construction can still be found. Dr Lewis refers to examples of half-timbered construction in the Maldon area and on French Island, and says that 'there is no limit either in Victoria or in Europe to

the number of permutations of half-timbered construction — that is, of timber frames with the panels filled with mud and other materials'.[2] Cottages at Yandoit, for instance, although in a ruinous state, show a unique variation of this method of construction in that the horizontals are fixed on either side of the posts as if acting as crude formwork for the mud in the middle. On Phillip Island the use of mud in a framework was traditional right into this century. A chicory kiln was constructed like this, and farm outhouses can still be seen opposite Rhyll, their walls made of mud and buckshot gravel between local saplings. Exford homestead near Melton is constructed of huge vertical logs on a basement wall of solid bluestone. The panels between the logs are lath and plaster. Many variations of wattle and daub can be found through the gold towns.

Some houses were built of adobe (Spanish) or clay lump (English) construction which consisted of sun-dried mud bricks mixed with chopped straw. Houses built like this can be found in North Harcourt and other places. In recent years there has been a revival of this method in the Eltham area, where the earth is of the right consistency. With its insulation properties, this material fits the low energy concept of building and current simple life style philosophy.

Pisé, or pisé-de-terre, an ancient method of wall construction well-known in France, consists of loam or puddled clay rammed between formwork. Cob construction differs from this in that lumps of mixed clay,

9

bourne. These were of fine quality clay and shallow in depth. Many of them were marked in opposite corners by a thumb print. There were other markings which served as a sort of trade mark for the brickyard. It has been suggested that one in every thousand were marked so that a rough tally could be made, but further research is required on this subject.

straw and water are applied in the plastic state without the use of formwork. Little of this, of course, has survived, but an example of the latter can still be found at Bear's Castle at Yan Yean.[3]

In a diary entry in 1837, Governor Bourke noted that there was good brick earth available; stone, though not of a good quality for building; timber at a distance of about eight miles; and limestone near Point Nepean. These were basic materials and the early builders made use of them within the limits of their technology.

But for the first buildings some of the materials were imported. The brig *Stirlingshire* arrived in Hobson's Bay in 1836 with Robert Russell, the architect, on her passenger list, thirty private soldiers, thirty convicts and a 'large quantity of timber and, amongst other things, 10,000 bricks'.[4] Bricks from the Port Arthur brickyards may also have found their way to Mel-

There were bricklayers among the convicts. William Buckley had been a brickmason and later a soldier, and built chimneys for John Batman. Mark Twain commented that Melbourne's 'first brick was laid and its first house built by a passing convict'.[5] There was a clay pit where Little Collins Street now runs and another in Flinders Street.[6] Bricks were made in that area now known as Alexandra Gardens and later in numerous kilns on the swampy flat

10

Exford homestead, near Melton (1842), is constructed of huge box logs on a bluestone substructure. The walls between these timbers are a variation of wattle and daub. The dormers would be familiar to settlers from Britain at that time

Bear's Castle, Yan Yean (1847). Built on the estate of Thomas Bear, this unique structure is, according to Miles Lewis, 'the only known pure cob structure in Victoria'. The mud walls rest on a masonry plinth and consist of lumps of mixed clay, straw and water having been applied in the plastic state without formwork. The walls were built up in layers which are clearly visible in this photograph

between the Yarra and Emerald Hill. John Jones Peers set up his brickworks in Richmond in 1846. Bricks were being made in Hawthorn by 1848 and W.H. Phillips and John Glew established brickworks in Brunswick in 1849, and throughout the country brick earth was usually dug from the site near the appropriate building operation.

The local bricks were fired in rough kilns, the heat being slowly built up with any timber to hand. They were soft and porous because of insufficient heat, underburnt, lacking in density, and their inability to withstand stress led to many structural failures. Generally, those made beside the Yarra were described as being of blue clay, weighing about four and a half pounds (two kilograms) and having a tendency to absorb moisture and fall to pieces. A resident of Brunswick recalled the primitive method of manufacture:

> My earliest recollection of brick-making was the breaking down in the pit of the soft yellow clay, lumps of which were carried by boys up a plank to be pressed into moulds. Then came the pug mill and winding gear, with small trucks on a tramway worked by horses. As the pit deepened, the reef appeared, and this brought into use the rollers to crush it and bring it into a plastic condition.[7]

The Lindsay brothers were making bricks in Brighton (see Chapter 1), and by mid-century in the low-lying area of Prahran brick-making flourished with Hart and Preston in Chapel Street, Sam Orton in Commercial Road and Daddy Davis on the

corner of Toorak Road and Chapel Street.[8]

Imported bricks were available but were too dear except for chimney and arch work. One problem was compression, and as compressing machinery became available the quality and density of local bricks improved and the weight of the early brick was nearly doubled. Another problem was workmanship. Builders habitually did not wet the bricks enough before laying. Some bricks with too much organic matter in the mix

tended to turn green with fungus growth. The redder bricks from the Castlemaine, Bendigo and Taradale areas we value highly today and expose for their colour and hand-made texture. In the early days they were often protected with render because of their porosity.

Bluestone was more permanent. It was first quarried in what is now Fitzroy Gardens and later in North Melbourne. Stone from a Footscray quarry was used for

11

Mandalay, 24 The Strand, Williamstown (1858-59), architect William Bull. A house designed by a local architect and built with local materials. The access road used to be on the left of the house

paving in Bourke Street and for the early jetties in Williamstown. Quarries opened up in Brunswick, Newport, Spotswood, Footscray, Yarraville, Clifton Hill and various locations west of Williamstown. Bluestone became a basic and traditional material for Melbourne, and when the quarries opened up at Malmsbury it was used for the bridges and viaducts on the railway lines to Ballarat and Bendigo. This continued through the century, and even in 1909 the *Footscray Advertiser* commented that 'the supply of stone is practicably inexhaustible, and that its merits for building purposes are recognized is shown by the fact that most of Melbourne's leading architects usually specify Footscray stone for use in foundations, etc'.

One of the leading architects, John George Knight, in a treatise on building stones in 1859 (subsequently published overseas) described the durability of bluestone as unquestionable and referred to Geelong sandstone, by comparison, as 'little more than indurated clay'. Bluestone was used extensively as base structures, wider blocks at foundation level forming a sort of strip footing. Thus we find it used under St James's Old Cathedral supporting a stone superstructure, under St Jude's, Carlton (to mention one of many) supporting a brick superstructure, and under the Congregational Church Hall in Stevedore Street, Williamstown, supporting a timber superstructure. It was standard practice to incorporate a slate damp-proof course just above ground level.

We can see a progression both in the

12

Invergowrie, Coppin Grove, Hawthorn. Built by James Palmer in 1846, this historic home reflects the English cottage orné fashion of that time. This is a view of the original cottage, which is a good example of early bluestone work with a touch of Romanticism

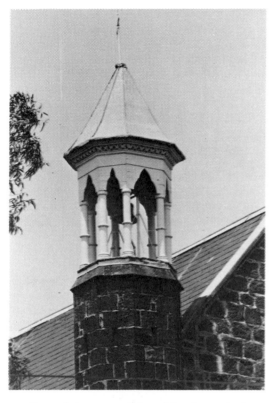

quality of the material and in the technique of using it. Consider Invergowrie, Coppin Grove, Hawthorn, for instance. When James Palmer built the original cottage in 1846 he used walls of random rubble, and the contrast is apparent between this and the extensions of 1869 where the masonry is coursed. The early work is coarse honeycombed bluestone which resulted from the rapid cooling of the lava flow; the later work is dense stone quarried from a deeper

level. Early bluestone work can be seen at The Hawthorns, Creswick Street, Hawthorn (1845); Christ Church, Hawthorn (architect Charles Vickers 1853); and Bishopscourt, East Melbourne (architects Newson and Blackburn 1853). The last two contracts were beset by labour problems because of the rush to the diggings.

Random rubble was used for Cobb and Co.'s depot on the corner of Spring and Lonsdale Streets (now demolished). Blue-

stone was used for all the early warehouses in Flinders Street and Flinders Lane near the old port of Melbourne. It was used in a charming and unsophisticated way in the little single-story houses, one-room-and-a-corridor wide, in Williamstown. It was used in one of the oldest houses in Victoria, Wentworth House, in Le Cateau Street, Pascoe Vale South (1840-41), where the basalt was found locally. It was supreme in engineering work. The foundation stone for

13

Christ Church, Hawthorn, designed by Charles Vickers in the early 1850s. This bell turret finishes with a timber structure of unsophisticated charm

La Rose, now called Wentworth House, 22 Le Cateau Street, Pascoe Vale South (1840-41). Built for Dr McCrae, this is reputed to be the second oldest house in Victoria and is referred to in 'Georgiana's Journal' of 27 April 1842. The original section is in the centre and right wing and is built of random volcanic rubble, locally found

the first Prince's Bridge, laid in 1846, came from Jonathon Lilley working an early quarry at Yarraville. He also supplied the pitchers laid in Elizabeth Street. At the Franco-British Exhibition of 1908 a dressed block of basaltic rock from the bluestone quarries of Footscray won a gold medal.[9]

Being dull and sombre in character and expensive to work, bluestone was often used so that the mouldings, window dressings, especially jambs, and quoins were formed with a different, contrasting material like brick or sandstone. This produced quite a charming effect.

Sandstone of a good quality was hard to find and, until the opening up of the Waurn Ponds quarries, was often brought in from Tasmania or Bacchus Marsh; but this was expensive (a price list of 1859 shows Bacchus Marsh stone to be 6s 6d per cubic foot as against local bluestone for 3s 6d). Local (Flemington) ferruginous sandstone was used for the walls of St James's Old Cathedral when it was originally built off William Street in 1839-40 and also for the Melbourne Gaol. In this early pre-gold rush period many buildings were constructed of local sandstone. Among these could be listed Schramm's Cottage, in East Doncaster (1850), Schwerkolt's Cottage in Nunawading (1860s), Black Rock House (stable courtyards 1856), Grove Church, North Box Hill (1856), Holy Trinity Church, Doncaster (1868-69) and the hall at the rear of the Methodist Church on the corner of Bell Street and Sydney Road, Coburg (1849). These all arose from their own environments in an unsophisticated way.

Timeball Tower, Williamstown, standing on what was called Point Drake. The lower bluestone structure was built by John Linacre in 1852. A large copper ball was lowered on a mast at 1 p.m. each day to allow masters of ships moored offshore to correct their chronometers. This continued till 1926

14

The practice of importing heavy cargo as ships' ballast meant that there were some interesting materials used in Melbourne's early buildings. Thus there was a church in Collins Street, where the Auditorium now stands, built of Caen stone from Normandy, and a garage in William Street built of white granite from China.

Matthew Flinders had commented that our timber was rarely sound and not large. It was plentiful—red gum, manna gum, stringybark and mountain ash—but although these were durable they were heavy, twisted in grain and difficult to work. In the Dandenong Ranges and further afield in the Great Divide there were magnificent stands of mountain ash suitable for masts and as structural timber, but access, milling and transport were expensive. There was no spanning timber to compare with oregon, so in the early years much was imported: teak from Singapore, oregon from America and pine from Europe. Nevertheless, sawpits were set up at an early date and by 1845 there were several steam-powered sawmills in Melbourne. English-trained architects and builders found themselves dealing with poorly seasoned Australian timbers and climatic conditions with which they were not familiar. Safety lay in imported timber. Consequently, by the mid-1850s timber imports were running at £100 000 ($200 000) per annum. In Melbourne joinery was usually quartered Baltic pine or oregon, but there are instances in the country of the use of 'best dry gum'.[10]

Local timber seems to have been little appreciated in the early years, except for rough work. An early specification refers to

15

Merrawarp (Honey's House), Ceres. William Honey came to Ceres to grow wheat and built this twelve-roomed house in the early 1850s with stone quarried from the site. In fact the building is carved out of a rock barrier and is an early and unsophisticated use of Ceres stone. The house is reminiscent of the current domestic architecture of Devon from which the Honey family emigrated

sleepers of gum to carry the floor joists, but the remainder of the timber was imported. A writer in the *Australian Builder* of August 1855 complained: 'We have scarcely commenced unfolding the vast wealth of our forests, but have been as foolish in this particular as we have as regards our necessary food — depended almost entirely upon other countries for supply'. He goes on to complain that 'we import quartering called 4 by 3 inches [100 by 75 mm] which will rarely even measure 3 by 2 inches [75 by 50 mm]'.

The 'balloon' frame from America was modified by Australian builders in a number of ways. They discarded the rough timber sheeting used for bracing and made the frame lighter and more stable by slim timber braces checked flush into the frame at the corners. Ceiling joists served to tie the feet of the rafters together, forming a simple triangle. At Gulf Station, Yarra Glen, for instance (c.1854), we find a simple roof construction of couples, tied at intervals by joists at ceiling level.

In those days (1850s) timbers were heavy by our standards: 6 by 3 inches (150 by 75 mm) floor joists at 18-inch (450 mm) centres and 5½ by 3 inches (137 by 75 mm) ceiling joists. Flooring was either rough timber slabs or, if sawn, at least 1¼ inches (31 mm) thick, secured by wrought brads. Timber advertisements in the press featured full-cut quartering, tongued Scotch flooring, American and Baltic deals, clear pine, red pine, yellow pine, oregon, hickory, ash, cedar, New Zealand pine, oak and assorted American lumber.

16

Weather and termites were persistent problems and builders were advised to carry out crude kiln-drying procedures over a charcoal fire, to treat their timbers with a hot solution of corrosive sublimate and to paint them with white lead and oil. With fairly primitive materials, Melbourne's first architects had to be resourceful.

Samuel Jackson found the timber unsuitable for structural purposes and not amenable to lengths of scantlings, but he used it for wattle-and-daub construction. He moved out to Sunbury where his brother was squatting. Here he made bricks of local clay and built a house near George Evans' Emu Bottom.

Like Exford homestead, Emu Bottom (1836) was a thing of beauty and simplicity created out of the discipline of crude materials in short supply. The Silurian stone was taken from the property and set in local (mud) mortar. Beams and fence posts were

2 Thompson Street, Williamstown (demolished), 1839. This was the house where the crew of the galley of Captain Gordon, the first Superintendent of Water Police, was quartered. It could well have been the oldest timber house in Victoria

17

A cottage at Yandoit (1860s). Although in a dilapidated condition, this is a fascinating essay in primitive materials, pealing off in layers. Like much of Yandoit, the wall is constructed of small volcanic rocks embedded in a muddy clay mortar and rendered over with a clay/sand mix retained by split saplings fixed between uprights of local timber

hand-adzed, the shingles were handsplit hardwood and the floors were mixed with ox blood and rammed hard. It was a sort of unconscious local language.

Many people overcame the problem of primitive resources by importing prefabricated houses. From the time of William Lonsdale, whose house was the first official residence, a steady stream of immigrants brought their houses with them. (Lonsdale's house was a product of the Royal Engineers and is still in storage in sections. After dismantling it was placed in the care of the National Trust. A complete inventory of its components survives.) John Pascoe Fawkner brought the frame of his six-roomed house from George Town to Melbourne in 1836 and the following year Thomas Napier, a carpenter from Scotland, brought his from Hobart. Dr Godfrey Howitt erected a house brought from England on the corner of Spring and Collins Streets in 1839.

In the same year Charles La Trobe arrived on the *Fergusson*, bringing his timber house, prefabricated in sections, with him. La Trobe bought 12 acres at Jolimont and sited his cottage near the corner of Agnes and Palmer Streets, facing the river. This cottage was moved to King's Domain in 1964 and carefully restored. At least one-third of the original plaster was saved, together with the handsplit lathing, and a few of the original bricks have been relaid. This was a modest home, possessing greater charm than the usual imported home of the period. In Williamstown there were cedar houses from China and Singapore and teak ones from India, but they have been added to and

An early example of a wattle and daub wall at Bacchus Marsh. Erosion by weather has made this type of construction very rare now

altered to such an extent that they are hard to identify.

Robert Russell was also an early arrival and was responsible for the layout of the town, later to be endorsed by Robert Hoddle. He designed St James's Old Cathedral (begun 1839), a church in the Wren–Gibbs–Hawksmoor classical tradition. It is noteworthy that Russell was once employed in the Edinburgh office of William Burn and then in the London office of the Regency architect, John Nash, and so was well grounded in classical form. Due to a disagreement with the building committee, he resigned in 1841 in favour of Charles Laing, who is responsible for the tower with its Byzantine motif. The church was finished in 1851 and served as Melbourne's cathedral for forty-four years. It is in the same tradition as the colonial churches of America and the work of Francis Greenway of New South Wales. The charm of St James's lies in the warm brown of its ferruginous sandstone, its interior design of artless simplicity and its tangible links with the pioneers of Melbourne.

One of the cedar box pews, which themselves are a great rarity from the past, has been enlarged by a slice being taken out of the bookrest to accommodate the opulent tomb of Edward Henty. There is a convicts' gallery with all sorts of initials carved into the cedar, two elevated vice-regal boxes, a curved altar rail of English oak and a marble baptismal font from St Katherine's Abbey, which was demolished at the start of Queen Victoria's reign to make way for a magnificent dockside building. St James's originally

St James's Old Cathedral, King Street, begun in 1839 and moved to its present site in 1913; architects James Russell and Charles Laing. This historic church is Melbourne's closest link with the earliest settlers. This view shows three basic materials: bluestone for the substructure, a warm brown sandstone for the walls and Tasmanian sandstone for the classical feature on the right

had two walnut pulpits, one of which can now be found in St Margaret's Church, Eltham.

Regrettably, and presumably due to rising land values, St James's was moved out of the heart of the city to its present site in 1913, the shape of the tower being altered in transit. This move explains the fact that at the sanctuary end there is an external Baroque feature in Tasmanian sandstone. Although this can hardly be seen from the

street now, it once prominently faced William Street.

Charles Laing's was the first fully set up architectural practice in Melbourne. He was City Surveyor from 1845 to about 1849.

The engineer David Lennox, who, like many others immigrating here during the gold rush, had been trained as a mason in Scotland, arrived in Melbourne from New South Wales in 1844. The first bridge in Melbourne, a simple timber structure

known as Balbirnie's Bridge, built for £400 ($800), spanned the Yarra a little to the east of the present Prince's Bridge. Lennox replaced this in 1846 by designing a single elliptical stone arch, 150 feet (46m) in span. This bridge, of which there are many photographs and lithographic prints still extant, was similar in feeling to his Lansdowne Bridge (1838) in New South Wales, which until recently carried the traffic of the Hume Highway. In length of span

20

The first Princes Bridge, designed by David Lennox and opened in 1850. This lithograph shows the opening ceremony. We may regard this as the last of the great masonry arches before the era of iron and steel

the arch was second only to the centre arch of London Bridge and three feet (90 centimetres) lower at the keystone. Opened by Superintendent La Trobe in 1850, it was to last for thirty years. David Lennox has been described as

a quiet modest man, a good tradesman and practical designer, with a talent for managing men and getting the best out of them. His bridges, simple in design, aesthetically excellent, and always suitable for their purpose, are monuments to a fine craftsman.[11]

This early period was one of slow development using simple materials, with a steady colonial tradition of good proportions and the right way of doing things. The Port Phillip settlement was still part of New South Wales and the economy of the young colony had been artificially boosted by extravagant land sales. The government's policy of land auctions which encouraged the buyer to retail in the same way had led to a spirit of speculation and gambling. Disastrous falls in the price of sheep and wool accelerated economic collapse and sheep men resorted to boiling down their stock for tallow. However, in contrast to the tranquil sheep runs around the future Ballarat and the Western District, the people were impatient for independence, and in the hills and creek beds shepherds and bullockies were stumbling across bits of gold. All this created an atmosphere of change, excitement and discovery.

A cast iron detail from Dr Coutt's Surgery, 231 Nelson Place, Williamstown (1851)

21

In the middle of the nineteenth century two events changed the course of history. First came the proclamation of Victoria as a self-governing colony, and then there was the discovery of gold in payable quantity.

The discovery of gold seems to have been official in the middle of 1851 in several places at once. There was Louis Michel in Anderson's Creek near Warrandyte, Esmond and Campbell at Clunes, and Thomas Hiscock at Buninyong. Two months passed before the rush was on and it was October before the news affected England.

The immediate result was sociological. The colony had been founded and fostered by the energy and patronage of a privileged aristocracy and squatter class, but now anyone might become rich overnight. New liberal and radical philosophies grew in the heady atmosphere and this gave rise to Governor Gipps's fear that they (the privileged) might have their throats cut. Though, to be sure, the immigrants who had already come to Australia were to a large extent from the labouring classes of the new industrial areas and tended to be radical in politics and responsive to change, adjusting to it more readily than the privileged classes.

The effect on architecture was a stoppage on building contracts through loss of labour to the goldfields, and similar problems affected all professions and occupations (there was only one doctor, for instance, for the whole town at the peak of the rush). With the value of gold at £3 an ounce ($6 for 28 grams), men of adventure rushed to the gold-fields and women in Melbourne

Chapter 3

Melbourne after the Gold Rush

The English village during the first half of the Nineteenth Century was still able to provide an excellent type of colonist to new lands beyond the ocean. The men were accustomed to privation and to long hours of out-of-door work, and were ready to turn their hands to tree-felling, agriculture and rough handicraft. The women were ready to bear and rear large families.
G.M. Trevelyan, *English Social History*

were left without protection. Even at the diggings rape and robbery were commonplace. 'Horses were shod and harnessed with gold, bottles of the most expensive wine were used for games of skittles, cigars were lighted with five pound notes.'[1]

An official report to the governor stated that 'fifty out of fifty-five constables have determined to go to the goldfields'.[2] At the peak of the gold fever as many as 10 000 people arrived in Melbourne in one week.

One observer counted no fewer than eleven sails in sight on the bay, all Melbourne-bound.[3]

The Melbourne of 1854 was four times bigger than that of 1851. Gold meant there was real money around which could be spent on building. Over £75 million ($150 million) worth of gold was produced in Victoria in the 1850s. This wealth led to the creation of a city.

The town merchants rather than the landed aristocracy now had an opportunity to prosper, and retail trade flourished through servicing the needs of a restless population moving to and from the goldfields. In the mining areas themselves, accident and sickness brought work for doctors and apothecaries and the multitude of litigation cases occasioned by conflicting claims and deep mining at places like Ballarat attracted the legal profession. The town of Melbourne acquired a sense of independence, of identity and of civic pride. There was talk of a railway, that symbol of nineteenth-century progress and civilization; a library; a museum and a university. Due to the philanthropy of Redmond Barry the foundation stones of the library and the university were both laid in 1854 and the first matriculation examinations were held the following year.

There was no immediate effect on architectural style. Design was still monitored by a fairly solid tradition respecting the right use of materials—brick, stone, timber—and the correct proportions and detailing of windows, doors, chimneys and fireplaces. Buildings designed in the 1850s

Two shops in Parker Street, Williamstown, probably 1858. An interesting example of small shops in this early township, revealing above the oregon windows (originally shuttered) the original lettering

show this clearly. The building now owned by the Mental Health Authority, 300 Queen Street (1856), shows a quiet approach to street architecture and has a close link with eighteenth-century town house design. This is the nearest approach to a Hobart or even an English Georgian house, although London's fire regulations would not have permitted the wooden eaves.

Again, 35 Hanover Street, Fitzroy, illustrates this tradition in a simple town

24

house built in stone in a good middle-class area. It has a parapet concealing a double-hipped roof and was built in 1854 by E. Hills, a stonemason. Next to it two more two-storey brick houses with stucco facing were built in 1860.

This house and many others built in the mid-1850s highlight the most significant result of the gold rush, namely the immigration to the colony of many skilled tradesmen, especially bricklayers and

masons. Further, 80 per cent of the British migrants were literate. The effect of this on architecture was a marked improvement in trade practice. Thus we find skilled masonry on such houses in Fitzroy and on the gold fields, like Montrose Cottage in Ballarat (1856).

With the 1850s came an increased need for accommodation and the beginning of simple row, or terrace, housing in the newer suburbs of Melbourne. Royal Terrace in

This is a close-up view of a typical nineteenth century shop window, framed in timber and with three lights and arched heads

Mental Health Authority Building, 300 Queen Street (1856). Designed by an unknown architect for John Smith, this town house echoes the mid-Georgian tradition of good taste and street-front elegance which can be seen in Hobart

35 Hanover Street, Fitzroy (1854). A bluestone house first inhabited by Edward Hills, a stonemason. This is a good example of a town house in a middle-class suburb in mid-century Melbourne

Nicholson Street, facing Carlton Gardens, was built in bluestone between 1853 and 1858. This was a fashionable address, and the terrace is a reflection of the Regency terraces of London or Cheltenham but interpreted in a coarser material. Terraces were an adaptation of the English pattern which had been worked out in a country where land was hard to come by. The terrace housing of early Melbourne was not limited to providing cheap housing for the working class (though this was certainly one of its functions), wealthy squatters and graziers had town houses also in the terrace style. Builder or investor saw the terrace house as a speculative venture and consequently cost was of prime importance. The maximum number of units per block of land produced the greatest profit. Economies were effected by party walls and the standardization of components, decorative features and finishes.

The average house of the period was built of brick and bisected by a passage running from front to back. On either side of the passage and at the front would be the dining and drawing rooms, then the bedrooms, followed by the kitchen and scullery at the end of the passage. A bathroom or washhouse might also be at the rear under a lean-to. Most of these houses were built by builder-speculators.

Imports included many labour-saving devices for the home. The cast iron bath became standard in larger homes, along with cooking stoves made in England and America and 'designed specially for the colonies'. Pine tubs, copper boilers and even washing machines made their appearance in the laundries, and in the kitchens ice chests and gadgets on the dresser were a foretaste of affluence from America. Most middle-class homes had a domestic servant whose work in the kitchen in hot weather was carried out contending with flies and poor ventilation.

In each building component there was a clear progression. The window, for instance, commenced with the twelve-light double-hung sliding sash, glazed with imported crown glass, and, with the importation of larger panes of Chance's sheet glass, gradually reduced its number of glazing bars till finally there was one pane to each sash.

Writing later in the century, Richard Twopenny commented on our buildings:

Architecturally speaking, there is little to admire. If the public buildings fail in this respect, the private houses have at

25

Royal Terrace, Nicholson Street (1853-58). An early example of simple row, or terrace, housing in what was once a fashionable address. This bluestone block of terrace housing has charm and dignity

least the advantage over them, that for the most part they do not pretend to any architecture at all. Many of the architects are self-taught, and have served little or no apprenticeship to the profession. Indeed, it should rather be called a trade, since they are often merely successful builders, who have taken to planning and superintending the erection of buildings, instead of erecting them themselves. This is one reason why private houses incline rather to the practical rather than to the beautiful. Another cause is the practical spirit of the colonists, which looks upon expenditure for mere ornamental purposes as wasteful and extravagant. Unless a man is really rich, he cannot afford the imputation of extravagance which any architectural expenditure will bring upon him.[4]

The general rise in the standard of construction and in domestic comfort from the mid-century onwards has been described and analysed in Robin Boyd's book *Australia's Home*. First gold, which, except for a few places like Ballarat, was not a continuing commodity, then wool and wheat brought Melbourne the prosperity which we shall consider in Chapter 5. Melbourne was entering the golden age of coaching, as Cobb and Co. extended its services and constituted a vital lifeline between the city and its hinterland where these riches were produced.

There was more permanence and dignity in the buildings, as seen in the Melbourne Club, 36 Collins Street, begun in 1858 and extended with a Collins Street frontage by Terry and Oakden in 1879. It has a dignified elevation in stucco, and the heavy application of architraves, cornices and pediments to each window and the use of large panes of window glass mark it out as typically mid-Victorian in style rather than Colonial or Regency. Leonard Terry was a pupil and employee of Charles Laing and in 1874 went into partnership with Percy Oakden. The partnership lasted till Terry's death in 1884. In 1887 the firm became Oakden, Addison and Kemp, whose story is taken up in Chapter 5.

The Club has a secluded garden at the rear alongside of a verandah reminiscent of a country homestead, and, according to Richard Twopenny, was

> the best appointed in the colonies. The rooms are comfortable, and decently, though by no means luxuriously, furnished, and a very fair table is kept. The servants wear full livery. There is a small library, and all the usual appurtenances of a London club, and a racquet court.[5]

In 1853 Bishopscourt was built in East Melbourne, but the contract suffered from the same labour shortage and price rises as others of the gold rush period. In fact Bishop Perry himself bought a cart for hauling the bluestone from Pentridge. Some other large houses were built in the mid-century—the original Broughton Hall in Camberwell, The Hawthorns in Hawthorn and Banyule in Heidelberg—using brick, stone and extravagant sizes of timber as scantlings—oregon, blackwood, boxwood, cedar and teak—often connected with pegs rather than nails, which were still in short supply. D'Estaville, 7 Barry Street, is grand with its rusticated bluestone which bears witness to the wealth of trade skills attracted to Victoria because of gold. At this time also, the entrance lodge of the Kew Asylum (Willsmere Hospital) was built amidst much opposition.

But the majority of houses were small and humble. In 1852 William Howitt described the view of the valley between Bishopscourt and the Yarra in *Two Years in Victoria* as

> that of an enormous extent of ground covered all over with thousands of little tenements, chiefly of wood, and almost every one of them of only one storey high. These extend as far as the eye can command the vale, the upper portion being called Collingwood and lower Richmond.

The smaller house was often prefabricated. At the time of the Great Exhibition of 1851, Britain had achieved international prestige in technology and acquired a worldwide market for manufactured goods. Engineering techniques, smelting, the manufacture and curving of corrugated iron, galvanizing and other processes were not only flourishing in England's industrial towns but later in Melbourne itself. (By 1856 3-inch (7.5 centimetre) and 5-inch

(12.5 centimetre) corrugation curving machines were operating in Little Latrobe Street and by 1859 John Carter of Little Bourke Street was operating a steam corrugating and curving works.) Prefabrication was viable not so much because Melbourne was technologically backward as because of the differential between local and overseas labour costs.

Further, the Crimean War created the need for prefabricated structures, buildings and bridges, to be shipped out to the Crimea, and when the war was over many of these were available for purchase. One bridge, for instance, was bought in 1856. It was fabricated in three sections, one of which spanned the Yarra at Prahran. This (Church Street) bridge was plagued by deflection and other problems until replaced in 1919-23 by a bridge designed by Desbrowe Annear and T. Ashworth, in conjunction with J.A. Laing.

The house at 189 Brunswick Street, Brunswick (c.1855) was designed, it is thought, as an administration building and has bullet-proof walls of corrugated iron. However, a curious feature of this house is the fact that internally the walls are brick, so we hesitate to call it a prefabricated house in the traditional sense. Its first owner was John Glew the brick-maker. Adjoining this on the south side are other houses of a similar nature and historically interesting, but they have had their cladding replaced or covered over. Ready markets for prefabricated houses followed the gold discoveries in the mid-century—California, New South Wales, Victoria, New Zealand— in that order. South Africa also shared in the market. For the vast numbers who increased Victoria's population a prefabricated house meant shelter.

To us, it is surprising that a prefabricated house of iron was acceptable at all, but we forget how desperate the situation was. Each successive shipload of immigrants was faced with a worsening situation. One settler, advised to stay in Williamstown because of the child mortality rate in Melbourne, rented two unfurnished rooms in a carpenter's house for £4 ($8) a week.[6] William Kelly, also arriving at Williamstown, referred to the 'prodigious rats' and 'sickening odours' there. 'As the people swept into the colony the problem was where to put them.'[7]

Every device imaginable was employed to provide accommodation. Even ships were used. On the south of the Yarra a canvas town to house 4000 to 5000 people was

27

Willsmere Hospital, Kew (1865-72). A view over the one-time Kew Asylum from one of the towers which were designed, but never used, for water storage. The layout was similar to that at Beechworth and other asylums, and the materials were local—stone for the substructure from Yarra Bend and six million bricks made on the site

erected. Costs of land and building soared; a comfortable cottage of four rooms which could have been rented for £30 ($60) a year in 1844 brought £300-£400 ($600-$800) a year in 1852.[8] A set of plans was prepared at the instance of a public committee in 1852 to provide shelter for 2000 homeless immigrants.

The newspapers of the day advertised prefabricated houses widely. 'Permanent houses built for exportation suitable to all the British colonies' was a typical advertisement. Henry Manning of Holborn made a business of manufacturing wooden houses in sections for use in Australia. He advertised a five-roomed house for £125 ($250), at two weeks' notice, plus £30 ($60) for freight out. John Tredwen was selling prefabricated wooden houses from the hulk *Protector*, beached along the Strand, Williamstown, near the foot of Fergusson Street, and the *Williamstown Trade Circular* in 1855 adver-

tised that two buildings were for sale, one 20 by 16 feet (6.0 by 4.8 metres), with three rooms, and the other 16 by 12 feet (4.8 by 3.6 metres).

A little timber house still in use, 3 Cox's Gardens, Williamstown (1851-53), its internal lining made from the packing crates in which it was imported, was of the above category. Houghton, 120 Princess Street, Kew, still stands as a four-roomed cottage, though added to at the rear. It was constructed of oregon and probably shipped from America in the 1850s. In 1853 there were many timber houses imported from England, America and Canada and, in addition to these, 6369 iron ones.[9] On the site of the Metropolitan Meat Market in North Melbourne there was an early exercise in prefabricated accommodation for new arrivals. A boarding house called the Club House, or Noah's Ark, designed to accommodate 200 to 300 persons, was shipped complete from England. Internally, on the ground floor, it was fitted with cabins all round the building, similar to those of a sailing ship. A balcony ran round the building on the inside. It was reached by stairs and had cabins around similar to those below.[10]

Peter Johns (fresh from the Crystal Palace in England and calling himself 'Iron House Erector') began to assemble iron houses in Fitzroy using imported materials. The emergency created the demand. While, in the emergency, iron houses were preferred to the rude comfort of local construction, it was soon found that they were insufferable in conditions of severe heat and

189 Brunswick Street (c. 1855). This is a strange mixture of prefabricated iron construction and internal walls and chimneys of brick

cold. But costs were on their side and local importers could undercut the price of a traditional house. The landed price on the jetty of a two-roomed iron house was sometimes as low as £25 ($50) and this would be bought within the hour for £70 ($140). A writer in 1899 said: 'The profit on some transactions in those days seems now almost incredible'.[11]

Following the Californian gold rush of 1849 there was a boom in the export of iron buildings, and the effect on architecture was to establish corrugated iron rather than the more organic materials as traditional and ubiquitous throughout Victoria. It become indispensible for all types of structures. 'It is difficult to exaggerate the technical importance of the development of corrugated iron, of galvanising, and of systematised prefabrication in the decade 1840-1850.'[12]

The original Emerald Hill was the home of many portable buildings of wood, iron and zinc. Several iron houses were erected in Patterson Street, South Melbourne[13] and in other inner suburbs, but few remain. These few include 59 Arden Street, North Melbourne, previously mentioned 189 Brunswick Road, Brunswick, and 399 Coventry Street, South Melbourne. On the latter site the National Trust has restored two houses. The one on the street frontage with a small attic was made in 1854 by John Walker of London and the one behind, by E.T. Bellhouse of Manchester, has an interesting variation in construction as the corrugations, running horizontally, are housed into special corner posts. Loren, also probably by John Walker, was a two-

storeyed house once in Curzon Street, North Melbourne, and now re-erected in the Moe Folk Museum.

At his Clift House Works in Bristol, Samuel Hemming was manufacturing a variety of iron buildings for export and Andrew Handyside and Company were able to supply iron buildings suitable to any specific purpose and were offering assistance in designing and detailing such structures. A two-roomed zinc house was

bought by the Church of England in 1853. With its centre wall removed it formed a room 40 by 14 feet (12.2 by 4.3 metres) and became St Mary's, North Melbourne, known locally as the Dutch Oven. It was replaced in 1860 by Lloyd Tayler's church which we see today. Handysides were offering roofs of two layers of iron with an air space between for insulation in hot climates. Their method of planning, using an equal module, was an early example of

A prefabricated iron house in Coventry Street, South Melbourne (1854), typical of many imported from London at that time. Notice that the corrugations are much wider than those of the iron produced locally later in the century

industrialized building techniques. Several warehouses were erected in Geelong, and Coppin's Royal Olympic Theatre, to seat 700, was erected in Lonsdale Street in six weeks.

Holy Trinity, Williamstown, was an iron church, the first of several sent out in the 1850s 'to supply the needs of public worship to the diggers'.[14] The manufacturer was Samuel Hemming. It comprised a nave, two side aisles, with pulpit, reading desk, baptistry, vestry and a tower. The outside lining was galvanized corrugated iron and the inner lining was canvas and felt. Its cost, apart from erection, was £1000 ($2000). Similar churches were sent by bullock waggon into the country. One was erected at Gisborne in 1855 and served as St Paul's for ninety-four years. It is now used as the Parish Hall in an emaciated condition. In the account of his travels in the Western District James Bonwick refers to the 'Zinc Church' near Port Fairy.[15]

Prefabrication is a broad term and it is not known to what extent parts of some houses were prefabricated. St Ninian's, Brighton (now demolished), probably received its wing facing the sea in the 1840s as prefabricated sections from Singapore and, with the development of the timber-framed structure it was soon possible to transport frames for houses or schools into country districts by waggon. The oak-panelled chapel at Overnewton Homestead at Keilor was brought from Scotland in 1859.

Not all prefabricated houses were small. Corio Villa was claimed for a song off the

Geelong wharf and assembled without instructions at Eastern Beach, Geelong, in 1856. The finest prefabricated house in Melbourne is surely Tintern in Toorak. This was erected in 1855 on a site of 105 acres (42.5 hectares). The original part of the house, including the bow-fronted drawing-room, is an imported iron structure. The walls are plastered on the inside as in-situ work but externally are three-quarter-inch (18 millimetre) iron plate. The windows are framed externally by architraves in the

mid-Victorian manner, and on closer inspection we find that these are iron. Even the shutters are quarter-inch (12 millimetre) boiler plate.

Avoca Lodge in South Yarra (now demolished) was another house of the period (c.1855). This had gables and a lacy verandah design, and could have been fabricated in America.

Those structures, built mainly of the resources of the land, have proved more permanent.

St Ninian's, Miller Court, Brighton (demolished). Built in 1841 by George Ward Cole on land bought from Henry Dendy, this house was a charming example of early cottage design in timber

31

*Como, South Yarra (1855), the best example of a
two-storeyed colonial house in Melbourne. The
basically Georgian elevation, the cast iron verandah
and the landscaping all speak of an extreme elegance*

Mandalay, 24 The Strand, Williamstown, was built in 1852 on a foreshore of low scrubby white mangrove and basalt boulders. The walls were 18 inches (45 centimetres) thick, of two skins of bluestone filled with rubble, shingle and mortar, the sand being from the beach. The architect was William Bull. Concurrently other two-storey houses such as 1 Yarra Street, 6 Hanmer Street and 27 Lyons Street were being built in Williamstown, where convict labour was plentiful.

Como Park used to be a billabong of the Yarra and was once an Aboriginal Protectorate. David Hill built a cottage there in 1839. William Lonsdale and his two nephews, Alfred and George Langhorne, named this run south of the Yarra 'Pur-ra-ran' (Prahran). Edward Eyre Williams bought the property in 1846 and called it Como, probably building the ground floor of the present house in 1847. The property changed hands to F.W. Dalgety and then to John Brown, who had been in partnership with Thomas Napier as a builder in Scotland. (Napier had featured in the first Melbourne land sales.) Brown completed the house except for the ballroom in 1855, the ballroom wing being added in 1874 for Charles Armytage, according to the design of Arthur Johnson.

This simple, gracious homestead with its foil of a two-storeyed verandah and cast iron lacework is rare in Victoria because most of the great homes were built in a later, more eclectic, period when influences and mannerisms from overseas were used to display wealth. Como, Armytage House in

Pakington Street, Geelong (1858-59), the Hepburn homestead at Smeaton (Smeaton House (1849-50) and one or two in the Western District are among the few that could be called 'colonial', akin to those of New South Wales and Tasmania. Como is a tangible link with Victoria's great pastoral wealth on which the colony's future prosperity was founded. As the National Trust Guide says, 'to walk here is to span a hundred years in a hundred yards, and arrive at

the threshold of an era already becoming magically remote'.

Its neighbour, Toorak House, was built by James Jackson in 1849. (In those days the grounds of Como, Grey Lodge and Toorak House occupied most of Toorak.) Toorak House was probably the first house with a dominating square tower (with a view over the Yarra valley). Its most attractive feature is the simple Doric colonnade. Restraint is the keynote and the absence of

32

Overnewton homestead, Keilor (1849-59). This photograph shows clearly the constrast between the early colonial homestead with its simple verandah and the later Scottish baronial style built after William Taylor, its first owner, returned from a visit to Scotland

Italian extravaganza is noteworthy. The quoins on the corners and the treatment of cornices with classical detailing set this building in the Regency-Picturesque tradition, and the verandah details with their cast iron lace, which was added later, supply the colonial touch.

At Waldau (East Doncaster) a settlement of German Lutherans developed in the early 1850s (see Chapter 1). Friedensruh in Victoria Street (1844) was originally a two-roomed wattle-and-daub cottage with a cellar. John Finger's home in George Street was built with bricks made on the site, and Max Von Schramm's cottage (since re-sited) is built of stone quarried from Ruffey's Creek.

In the same spirit of vernacular or organic architecture, August Schwerkolt built his cottage in Deep Creek, Mitcham, using materials locally available—stone and mud from the creek, young trees as verandah posts and bricks from one of the many kilns in Mitcham at that time. Like the Lutheran settlements in the Barossa Valley this is an instance of Europeans using construction techniques with which they were familiar, only with colonial modifications, like the verandah round Schwerkolt's Cottage.

In that critical year of history, 1851, the Victorian Architects' Association was founded with the object, amongst others, of 'upholding architecture in this colony in its proper rank as one of the polite professions'. Its members included Charles Laing, James and Charles Webb and Samuel Jackson.

33

Toorak House, Tahara Road, Toorak (1849 or 1850). Built for James Jackson, the original estate stretched from Toorak Road to the river. Between 1854 and 1875 it was the residence of five Governors. A gracious house without any of the later Italianate extravagances

Five years later, through the energy of Thomas Watts and T.J. Crouch, another body was formed. Known as the Victorian Institute of Architects, it was described by its first president, John George Knight, as 'an animated body, having a higher aim than the assertion that five per cent is a reasonable and proper remuneration for an architect's services'.[16] Knight was active and influential in the profession right through the century. The aim of the Institute was 'the cultivation of friendly intercourse between the members of the profession—the protection and advancement of its interests, and the elevation of architecture as an art'.

To them architecture was primarily an art, only distantly related to the developing technology and the needs of the community. A proposed amalgamation with the civil engineers did not materialize.

Guided by a council consisting of Peter Kerr, Albert Purchas, A.L. Smith, Thomas Watts and F.M. White, there were many competent architects in the membership. However, the Institute was somewhat inward-looking and preoccupied with the rules. Professionalism was important, and the extent of an architect's services, who should own the contract documents and regulations regarding competitions. It was due to the infringement of the latter relative to the Eastern Market Building that Reed and Barnes were expelled in 1877.

Victorian standards of respectability permeated the Institute and the ultimate disgrace was to be struck off the roll. This is what happened to Charles Selby after being in the Police Court for indecent exposure. Alfred Dunn advertised his services thus: 'Those about to build will save 25% by employing Alfred Dunn A.V.I.A.'. This was thought to be of an 'objectionable and touting character' and he was let off with a warning letter.[17]

In those days each building type had a fairly conventional symbol or outward appearance in the built environment. Meaning and symbolism required little rethinking among architects. Each building type, whether a church, school, court house or gaol, had definitive characteristics.

Thus, the Melbourne Gaol on the corner of Russell and Franklin Streets reflected the conventional idea of a Victorian gaol, and there was no doubt about the need for one. Even before the gold rush the western end of Little Collins Street became 'the scene of nightly brawls that soon gave to Melbourne, while still but a pretty country town, one at least of the features of a great metropolis, and that the most odious'.[18]

The first gaol had been built on Government Block in 1838 and had to be enlarged in 1840, the enlarged premises being fully occupied almost immediately. In 1841 a new out-of-town site was chosen, where the gaol now stands 'among the gums and she-oaks' (Garryowen). Lonsdale Street in those days was the line of demarcation between town and country. The citizens were alarmed at seeing such a large gaol being built. A wall 20 feet (6 metres) high was added later and the gaol was opened in 1854. Building work was completed in 1862 and demolition was started in 1880.

Today, only three parts remain intact—a three-storey cell block, the main entrance through a magnificent bluestone arch and the chapel which is now used by Emily McPherson College. The Royal Melbourne Institute of Technology acquired part of the land and, during excavation for building, dug up skulls in an area which had been used for burials. Whilst the cell block is forbidding enough, the main entrance and chapel have a touch of Baroque grandeur reminiscent of the work of Francis Greenway.

Collins Street Baptist Church is in the tradition of non-conformist architecture and is virtually a preaching hall for non-liturgical services. A little group of Baptists met in a tent in 1838 on land owned by Thomas Napier, now occupied by the Regent Theatre. The present church building was begun by John Gill in 1845 and extensively altered and enlarged by Joseph Reed in 1856 to hold 1000 people. He added the tetrastyle portico in 1862. The flight of steps was made necessary after the regrading of Collins Street later in the century.

The classical facade seems to have set a pattern for early Baptist churches, as seen in Albert Street, East Melbourne; the church on the corner of Chapel and Wilson Streets, Prahran, no longer used as a church; and the Baptist Church in Ballarat West. The first-named is worth comment. Albert Street Baptist Church was designed by Smith and Watts in 1859 and had seats for 700 'placed in the same manner as in the French Chamber of Deputies—that is to say—in a semi-circle and rising one above

Collins Street Baptist Church (1845-62). Designed by John Gill and enlarged by Reed and Barnes, this is typical of a powerful Renaissance statement in street architecture in contrast to Gothic. There is simple geometric harmony of proportion here

the other from close to the minister's reading desk up to the walls of the church'.[19] Its crowning glory was a Finchams organ installed in 1877.

Another non-Gothic church of great significance is Christ Church, Brunswick, designed by Purchas and Swyer in 1857. This was a simple aisleless nave, roofed with a series of timber trusses. It was enlarged by Smith and Watts in 1863-64 with the addition of transepts, chancel and vestry. The same architects added the campanile in 1870-71, and J. Wyatt the apse in 1874-75. The church was designed from the start in what was then called the Italian manner, though to what extent the original architects envisaged the campanile in its present position is not known. Today we would refer to it as Italianate, or, more accurately, Lombardic Romanesque. (Lombardy was a source of inspiration to many Melbourne architects in the late nineteenth century.) The feature which speaks prominently of this is the detached campanile, linked to the church by a small porch.

Built of local Brunswick brick in the days when the area was known as Phillipstown, the church is beautifully controlled by the campanile, which effortlessly dominates the composition. It is a rare thing in Victoria, the only other example known to the writer being St Columba's Church in Lydiard Street North, Ballarat. Two further points are worth mentioning here. Firstly, a builders' pattern book entitled *Villa Rustica* reached Australia in the 1840s and was promoting this (admittedly domestic) style. Secondly, the first incumbent of Christ

Church, Charles Bardin, who, like the Vicar of Bray, remained for the best part of half a century, came from Boswell in Tasmania. Between Boswell and Hobart there are two churches of this style, and Bardin could have been the initial stimulus and stabilizing influence behind the development of this church.[20]

At this time some of Melbourne's great public buildings were commenced, giving to the city some of the richest examples of Victoriana in the world. The Treasury Building (1857) was probably designed by John James Clark, a young draftsman in the Public Works Department. Built to hold the gold from the mining towns, the ten vaults in the basement have outer walls a foot (30 centimetres) thick and doors of solid iron. These walls below street level are structurally interesting because of the inverted relieving arches between the piers. A lot of unkind things were said about this building in newspapers of the day, but its timeless qualities are unanswerable. There is a fine sense of composition and depth of modelling, especially in the arched loggia on the first floor, and the rustication of the wall surface is reminiscent of the Strozzi Palace in Florence. The drawings which are kept in the Public Record Office show how painstakingly the details were worked out. The high branched cast iron lamp standards, added in 1867, add distinction to the monumental sweep of the front steps to the terrace.

Clark was probably responsible for the Royal Mint (1869) in William Street (now the Civil Marriage Registry) and did impor-

Albert Street Baptist Church (1859). Designed by Smith and Watts, this is a rare example of a church for Noncomformist worship at that time, with its circular arrangement of seats contrasting with the classical street facade

Above: Christ Church, Brunswick, the campanile, designed by Smith and Watts in 1870-71. This is a powerful controlling feature of the church in the Italian Lombardic manner, the contrast from the usual being accentuated by the Gothic spire in the background

Right: Treasury Building, Spring Street (1857-62). Architect probably J.J. Clark of the Public Works Department. Built of brick, bluestone and Bacchus Marsh freestone, this building, with its powerful arcaded motif seen here in close-up, shows the results of fine workmanship by craftsmen attracted to Melbourne by the gold rush. 'Melbourne's most elegant building', according to a press report of the day

37

*Civil Marriages Office (once the Royal Mint),
William Street, 1869-72, designed by the Public
Works Department (probably J.J. Clark). This is a
Renaissance facade in the grand manner, modelled in
stucco which had been the Regency fashion. This
building, which contains a geometrical staircase in
bluestone, has been finely restored*

tant work in Queensland, New South Wales and also in New Zealand. In the next century he and his son, E.J. Clark, designed the Melbourne Hospital in Lonsdale Street (now the Queen Victoria Hospital). In many ways Clark's career resembled that of William Mason, who left a career in London for New Zealand in 1840. He also was in public service, and it was said that others might 'envy Mason's opportunities in his various fields, but they must admire the

These photographs show something of the rich Renaissance detailing and craftsmanship involved around each window of this building

way he grasped them. He was the exemplary colonialist rather than the expatriate architect'.[21]

Melbourne Town Hall was commenced in 1867 to the designs of Reed and Barnes. (Joseph Reed will be mentioned more fully in Chapter 4.) The tower was added and named in honour of Prince Alfred, who visited the country at that time. The building sits on a bluestone base, the upper part being Tasmanian freestone. The shape

of the tower and classical detailing in superb masonry reflect civic pride and set the pattern to be followed by other town halls, notably North Melbourne, South Melbourne, Fitzroy, Collingwood and St Kilda. Those at Ballarat and Bendigo are just as magnificent.

Joseph Reed won the competition for the State Library, the foundation stone of which was laid in 1854, and the same firm (Reed and Barnes) was responsible for the building through all its stages of development. Reed's original building still faces Swanston Street, that is, the central block containing the magnificent Queen's Hall on the first floor and faced with a Corinthian octastyle portico. We could compare this with his porticoes on the Trades Hall in Lygon Street (1873) and the Geelong Town Hall (1855). The Victorian architect was supremely confident in handling these as much as he was with, say, Gothic arches and cusping; as competent, in fact, as the modern architect is in handling the principle of framing and cladding.

The Customs House, like Cole's Store and other warehouses now demolished, once looked out across Queen's Wharf when the ships could navigate the Yarra and tie up in Melbourne proper. The present building was built by Knight, Kemp and Kerr in 1858 and not completed till the 1870s. Like its equivalent in Williamstown, it is a good example of the 'official' style customarily used by the Victorians to represent the Establishment and all it stood for. Those were heady days, for alongside the growth of capitalism, government, of-

39

40

Melbourne Town Hall, Swanston Street, architects Reed and Barnes. The foundation stone was laid in 1867, and the top stone of Prince Alfred's Tower, seen in this photograph against a background of the Manchester Unity Building, was set in 1869. With its fine masonry it seems to epitomize Victorian Melbourne

ficialdom, customs and license inspections there was a very solid growth in the organization of labour, later to develop into unionism. Although these two forces had their tragic confrontation at Eureka, it should be recognized that after the mid-century in all these centres of growth—Melbourne, Geelong, Ballarat, Bendigo, Castlemaine—it was the rank and file of a very cosmopolitan labour force rather than any privileged squatter class

The Customs House, Flinders Street, begun 1858 and completed in the 1870s, architects Knight, Kemp and Kerr. This building once faced busy Queens Wharf and has a fine reception room on the first floor. In the 'official' stucco-covered style of the day, it has four magnificent elevations

A close-up of the Ionic order as used on this building on the rear elevation

41

that supplied the muscle, the sinew, the energy and the enterprise of the emerging community. And, as noted previously, after the gold rush this labour force had the trade skills and the education to produce fine building.

The Customs House building is fine and distinctive in many ways, being an 'all round' building. That is, the rear and side elevations are as carefully worked as the front. It was designed to be viewed from any angle and its vast and imposing Long Room, with its giant flanking Ionic colonnades, is one of the best enclosed spaces in Melbourne. Access to it was once by a lattice-enclosed hydraulic lift surrounded by a bluestone staircase. The lift has been removed.

Not all the warehouses have shared the fate of Cole's Store. One of the most imposing is that of Goldsbrough Mort on the corner of Bourke and William Streets. It was built of bluestone ashlar work by Charles Butler in 1861, with additions to the top floor and north end in 1882. Not only is the treatment of the walls impressive, but also the extravagant use of oregon in the floor structure. There are smaller structures built as warehouses in King Street, some of which have been successfully recycled as restaurants (e.g., Lazar's Restaurant, built in 1858).

Space forbids mentioning all these buildings, but Swallow and Ariell's Steam Biscuit Manufactory in Port Melbourne, built in 1854, should be noted. It is of three storeys and the facade is framed in by plinth, quoins and cornice. The windows are regularly spaced and the floor levels are picked out with string courses.

As in America at the same time, with uncontrolled immigration there was an exciting mixture of races. By 1854 there were 2000 Chinese in the colony, causing resentment in Bendigo and riots in Beechworth. The high point of Chinese immigration was reached in 1859, when statistics show that one in nine adult males was Chinese. With the decline of alluvial mining many Chinese took to fishing and market gardening. Those who returned to Melbourne from the diggings settled in Little Bourke Street and around the South Melbourne Market. The Joss House was built in 1866 in Raglan Street, South Melbourne, in the swampy area known as Emerald Hill. From earliest times the site was reputed to be lucky. The present building was to serve as the main centre of worship and the death registry for Cantonese in Victoria. With its centre block and two flanking 'pavilions' it is Palladian in composition, Italianate in its loggia treatment and oriental in its detail and atmosphere.

The Victorian landscape included the typical park with its European trees, its bandstand, its curiosities, its rare specimens and its emphasis on horticultural display, planned by men of vision and ability arriving with the gold-seekers. James Sinclair transformed a disused quarry into Fitzroy Gardens. W.R. Guilfoyle transformed the old bed of the Yarra into the Botanic Gardens, and left many a mark of his landscaping ability throughout the Western District. Ferdinand von Mueller arrived in 1852 and, as a tireless explorer and government botanist and foundation Director of Melbourne's Botanic Gardens, brought the city and the whole colony into worldwide repute in the realm of botany. He died in 1896.

Under such men, Melbourne developed as a garden city with reservations for parkland which can only now be fully appreciated because the trees have reached maturity.

The mid-century period was one of establishment and foundation-laying, of unpredictable change, excitement and discovery. On the one hand the cottages were built, the roots were going down and men were finding that fulfilment in the communities of a new country which would have been denied them in the class structure of the old. On the other hand, few things were staid, settled or routine and men were aware of the great unexplored country that stretched over the northern horizon. When Burke and Wills set off from Royal Park in 1860 the imagination of many went with them.

The Joss House, Raglan Street, South Melbourne (1866). Stone dogs guard this building forbiddingly. It has some oriental features and constitutes a historical link with the contribution of the Chinese to Victorian life. It has now been restored

43

The eighteenth century had been an age of order and reason. Art had been according to the rules of symmetry, and this applied as much to a phrase by Mozart as to a Palladian elevation. Towards the close of the century the movement known as Romanticism tended to disturb this ordered world. It affected all the arts, the poetry of Keats and Shelley, the drawings of Blake, the paintings of Turner and the music of Beethoven. Beethoven's ninth symphony was being performed for the first time in Vienna as Hume and Hovell were pioneering their overland route. To Melbourne's early citizens he was *avant-garde*. They brought with them the music of Handel and Mozart and the hymns of Charles Wesley. With them came also the piano, the reed organ and the brass band.

Antiquarianism and a nostalgia for the Middle Ages brought a revival of interest in Gothic architecture and a sentimental regard for ruins. Those who settled in Melbourne had been aware of the Romantic Movement in Europe and were stirred by the ideals of freedom, radicalism and spiritual audacity, expressing all this as they built not so much with the colonial homestead as the Gothic villa. This villa, or *cottage orné*, was the antithesis of the Palladian house, featuring an irregular plan, a display of individualism and a proliferation of picturesque gables. Generally, they did not need architectural services, for a builder could follow a pattern book, many of which were produced during the depression following Waterloo. (For example P.F. Robinson's *Designs for Ornamental Villas*

Chapter 4

Gothic Revival

Australian historians on the whole have underestimated the degree of churchgoing and church membership in the mid-nineteenth century and later.

Geoffrey Serle,
From Deserts the Prophets Come

and Village Architecture.) Like the Carpenter Gothic of New England, these gorgeous heresies with their decorative timber work were made by carpenters who drew strength from the good wood and scroll saws in their hands and their own skill.

In this early, or picturesque, period of Gothic Revival we see 'country' villas built by leading citizens after Melbourne had climbed out of its first depression. James

Denham Pinnock built The Hawthorns in 1845 and a year later James Palmer built the original two-storey cottage now known as Invergowrie. These two buildings, close to one another and to the early river crossing leading into Hawthorn, are both of bluestone and have similar features, including Tudor drip-moulds over the windows and decorated barge-boards. Invergowrie, as originally built, was a quite unsophisticated two-storey English cottage, with bell turret and storm porch. Its little 'gatehouse', on the corner of Burwood Road and Coppin Grove, has similar barges and a quiet charm like the rustic lodges and cottages which sprang up near the parks of great Gothic mansions in England. They seemed to fit into the countryside harmoniously and express an enviable world of Romanticism.

Victorian thought fostered much discussion on styles, and Melbourne was becoming known as the intellectual centre of Australia. As early as 1859 there was a leader in the *Australian Builder* questioning the validity of Gothic Revival. The writer attacked 'those gentlemen who think that Gothic architecture is the only mode of building to give us comfortable homes and weathertight roofs, picturesque exteriors and orthodox churches' and he traced the root cause of it all to John Ruskin. But cultured opinion was generally romantic and of the many house designs published in the building journals of that day the majority were picturesque, if not extravagantly so.

Ruskin was required reading for the architect of taste. What had started at

in the rectangular design of Collins Street Baptist Church and in the circular shape of the Independent Church on the corner of Collins and Russell Streets. On the other hand, the constructive elements of Gothic were intended for a special plan incorporating pillared aisles, transepts and chancel, a plan which ideally suited churchmen influenced by the Oxford Movement or the Camden Society. With few exceptions the Gothic was preferred and, even if the plan was essentially a preaching house, Gothic details and decorative motifs were attached to keep faith with sentiment and link up with traditional Christianity of medieval Europe. Even in the Gothic aisled churches those Victorians of evangelical beliefs saw the significance of a preaching house and placed the architect in a dilemma. In several cases he was able to dispense with the aisles and achieve one simple and impressive span. This was done by Reed and Barnes at St Jude's, Carlton (1866-70), and by Terry and Oakden at St Matthew's, Prahran (1877-78), where the clear span of its simple couple and collar roof is 45 feet (13.7 metres).

In many places the whole Gothic system was adopted, even by Methodists. 'Some of our friends are apprehensive that in the erection of these Gothic structures we are departing from the simplicity of original Methodism', said Daniel Draper, the minister of Wesley Church in Lonsdale Street. His influence led to the choice of Reed and Barnes' design out of sixteen competitors for the building of his church (1857-58).

Strawberry Hill, built for Horace Walpole at Twickenham, England (1750-70), as a picturesque fancy or a polite essay, developed into a religious exercise. The civilized, tolerant, Georgian view had been Gothic for romance, Classic for reason, but the Victorians associated classical architecture with paganism. Their revival of Gothic was not an academic exercise but a rediscovery of pure Gothic with moral and religious overtones. As Robert Furneaux Jordan said, 'Now, with Pugin, it [Gothic] became a means of grace, a way to salvation'.[1]

As we shall see, the influence of Pugin was unmistakable in the Gothic Revival of Melbourne. In church architecture there were two opposing requirements. The 'nonconformist' building required a large preaching area with an unrestricted view of a centrally placed pulpit. Reed and Barnes complied with this requirement successfully

The Hawthorns, Creswick Street, Hawthorn (1848). A bluestone house with walls 600 mm thick and squarely axed basalt at opening jambs and quoins. Scantling timbers are blackwood and boxwood. The spouting is cast iron and the flashings are lead. The verandah has been re-modelled in this century

45

The church is cruciform in plan and is built of bluestone with sandstone dressings. Draper told Reed that he wanted the most beautiful Gothic church he could design and during the course of construction was able to say: 'Our cathedral in Lonsdale Street is being roofed in. It is a splendid affair—the best in the colonies'.[2] It was Decorated Gothic yet shaped like one of Christopher Wren's London churches which were basically preaching halls. The same could be said of the Congregational Church in Howe Crescent, South Melbourne.

Decorated Gothic was the style current during the period of Merry England and has been described by John Betjeman as having 'windows large and divided into two or more lights by mullions, the tracery in the head geometrical or flowing ... mouldings bold and finely proportioned, the ball and four-leaved flower predominate; parapets pierced with quatrefoils and flowing tracery; niches, pinnacles, crosses, etc.'.[3] It was the age of spires, built over square towers to steady the weight of the bells as they rocked in the bell-chamber. Sometimes the base of the spire would incorporate triangular shapes to achieve the transition from the octagonal shape (on plan) of the spire to the square shape of the tower. These were called broach spires.

It was the style which, according to the Camden Society, better expressed the Christian ideal, but the idea was severely limiting. To attempt to reproduce the carvings and the tracery of fourteenth-century England with colonial workmanship and limited resources was not realistic; where,

46

St Jude's Church of England, Carlton. This simple one-span church on a bluestone base structure was designed by Reed and Barnes in 1866. 'The patterned brickwork is utterly charming today with its multi-colours, facetted and tuckpointed—skills of a bygone age' (Trust Newsletter, August 1972)

for obvious reasons, the frills were omitted, the design would be castigated in the press. If the style of, say, the Angel Choir at Lincoln were adopted for a secular building, the result would be incongruous and irrelevant. As Kenneth Clark commented: 'The strict limitation to the Decorated style has always seemed to be the greatest disaster which befell the Gothic Revival'.[4]

But the style had come to stay and continued into this century, culminating in the Cathedral of the Sacred Heart at Bendigo (1895-1977). It began with an emphasis on the picturesque and finished with an emphasis on the religious. It started with cottages and developed with churches. Its prophet was Augustus Welby Northmore Pugin, whose unsparing exposure of sham and insincerity brought a new moral concept into architectural design. Its teacher was John Ruskin, whose book, *The Seven Lamps of Architecture*, set forth the value of a building as depending not so much on technical competence as on the moral worth of its creator. This was new, but Victorian sentiment was deeply felt and the idea permeated the culture of the age. It was natural that the colonists should have brought the idea with them. But the 'idea' was simplified, Australianized, adapted to local conditions and robbed of some of its finesse. According to Hartley Grattan, the process of transplanting a culture from an old country to a new is an 'intricate process of establishing continuities, and engendering original contributions, from which a palpably original synthesis evolves'.[5] We shall see how this worked out in practice.

Samuel Jackson, architect and builder, seized his opportunities and had the qualities to contend with poor materials and unskilled pre-gold rush workmanship. Setting up office in Collins Street in 1840, he was responsible for St Francis's Church on the corner of Elizabeth and Lonsdale Streets. This was a modest Gothic structure divided into bays by simple buttresses. We can still detect five bays of his original brick church of 1841-45 and his cedar ceiling of 1849, but this has been overshadowed by more recent work. The Lady Chapel was added by George and Schneider in 1856 and finished internally by James Souter and Louis De Gould who had worked for Pugin. (To have 'worked for Pugin' was an impressive reference in those days.) The more overpowering sanctuary and front porch were added in 1878 by Reed and Barnes, incorporating an altar of marbles from Carrara, Levant, Sienna and other places.

Jackson went into partnership with Robert Russell for the Prince's Bridge competition, being placed second to David Lennox. He designed Melbourne's first hospital using a collegiate Tudor style. He also built Scots Church in Collins Street (1841) and St Paul's Church in Coburg in 1849.

Charles Laing was more professional and his practice was purely architectural. For each job he would issue proper documentation. His work can be seen in two churches still standing. He succeeded Robert Russell in the design, especially of the tower, of St James's Old Cathedral and is credited with the interesting elevation on the east end of

the church which, as already noted, originally faced William Street. He also designed St Peter's, Eastern Hill (1846), at least the original church consisting of the present nave. This structure, which was similar in feeling to St Francis's Church, was built of imported English bricks. (Many of such materials were carried as ballast.)[6] This stucco-faced charm is not shared by the later extensions forming choir and transepts added by Charles Vickers and Terry and Oakden later in the century. The early work including the tower reflects an economical ('churchwardens') form of Gothic resulting from the Church Building Act in England of 1814. However, in spite of its 'thinness', this building with its vicarage reflects the traditional, anonymous, village church design in England at that time.

John Knox Church, now the Church of Christ, in Swanston Street, was also Laing's design. It was built in 1847 facing Little Lonsdale Street, having a bell of very rich tone cast at Langland's Foundry in Flinders Street. The church we see today was built by Charles Webb in 1863, incorporating some of the soft bricks from the older church which subsequently gave trouble in weathering. Because of the defects of pre-gold rush brick manufacture, stucco was preferred for protection and a facing.

William Wardell arrived in Melbourne in 1858. That he had been a disciple of Pugin is only conjecture, but he knew his Gothic grammar and had a distinguished record, having designed thirty churches in England. Almost immediately he was commissioned

47

to design the 'third' St Patrick's Church in East Melbourne (or had he been commissioned before emigrating?). The question of Wardell's commission and the incorporation of the two earlier churches into his final design awaits further research. The foundation stone of the first church was laid in 1850—a sandstone building designed by Samuel Jackson. The second was by George and Schneider. But neither church was completed and both were extended

48

Church of Christ, Swanston Street (1863), architect Charles Webb. This replaced an earlier church by Charles Laing, from which some of the bricks were salvaged and reused. With its stucco finish and graceful trusses this is a good example of mid-Victorian Gothic

St Patrick's Cathedral, East Melbourne (1858-1939), architect William Wardell. Whereas St Paul's Cathedral reflects the character of Butterfield, this one reflects the soaring freedom of fourteenth-century Gothic

after some demolition. Of the first, probably only the foundations remained. Of the second, apparently the southern aisle remains except for one bay which was found to be 6 inches (15 centimetres) out of plumb. The west wall was rebuilt and an extra western tower was incorporated into the design. The north wall was pulled down and rebuilt with an extra aisle and by April 1859 three bays in the south aisle were ready for worship.[7]

Built of the dark bluestone of Footscray, St Patrick's was not finally complete until the three spires were built in this century. The sanctuary end, which is incredibly rich in craft skills and imported materials, especially marble, has a ceiling which shows the influence of Pugin clearly and is a marvellous essay in the handling of space and light. Light, the very essence of Gothic, plays on the stonework and penetrates this sequence of spaces with a masterly

presence. The plan is similar to that of Amiens Cathedral and is possibly the finest example of Gothic Revival anywhere in the world.[8]

The spires of St Patrick's were finally built in 1937-39, as re-designed by W.P. Conolly and G.W. Vanheems, with T.G. Payne appointed following the death of Vanheems. This revised design entailed an increase in the height of the central spire of 89 feet (27 metres) beyond that envisaged by

This view of St Patrick's Cathedral gives a good impression of the chevet, the complicated roofing pattern and the system of flying buttresses

49

Wardell. Consequently each of the four main piers of the crossing was underpinned for a footing of 16 feet (5 metres) square to take a load of almost 1000 tons (1020 tonnes). The spires were constructed of reinforced concrete and faced with Hawkesbury River freestone. The height of these spires and those of St Paul's Cathedral is one of the emotive characteristics of Victorian Gothic Revival. They are irreplaceable treasures in a modern computerized city.

In 1882 Wardell designed George Verdon's office and bank on the corner of Collins and Queen Streets (now ANZ). It is Gothic with fifteenth-century windows and Venetian flavour, reflecting the influence of Ruskin's *The Stones of Venice*. Built of Pyrmont freestone, this bank is superbly designed, incorporating blackwood counters, linenfold panelling and arches with cusping curving up from columns to a ceiling enriched with gold leaf within a banking chamber 67 feet (20 metres) long, 57 feet (17 metres) wide and 30 feet (9 metres) high. Wardell's building needs to be seen fronting a canal. Its sensitivity, restraint and plain wall surfaces can be readily appreciated by comparing it with William Pitt's Stock Exchange and Safe Deposit (now ANZ Bank building 376-380 Collins Street), built seven years later, which brings out all that is best, and worst, in High Victorian architecture. The detailing is marvellous but overall it is restlessly overplayed.

Wardell's other churches include St Mary's, Williamstown, (1859), St Ignatius, Richmond, the transepts for which were not

50

ANZ Bank, corner of Collins and Queen Streets (1883), architect William Wardell. Built of Pyrmont sandstone, this building is restrained and finely detailed. A touch of Venetian Gothic is evident in this (Queen Street) elevation and in the superb window and arcading details

Gothic arcading on the Queen Street elevation of Wardell's bank. Venetian in style, this is a superb device for providing depth and rhythm contrasting strikingly with the plain ashlar of the wall surfaces. The shadows of the bosses above are similar to those of dentils in a classical cornice

completed till 1889, and St John's, Toorak (1860-65). The latter is charming in its composition on a key site and incorporates the most artlessly simple broach spire in Victoria. It is not highly original, for Gothic Revival in Victorian times was fairly stereotyped and there are churches in England which are similar in feeling and detailing (e.g., St Mary's, Long Ditton by G.E. Street), but all these show the unmistakable influence of Pugin, who was the fountainhead of this prolific era of church building. Its simplicity and finesse speak in a silhouette sadly marred in competition with high-rise flats. Peter Staughton reported to the National Trust that it was 'perhaps the finest parish church design in this state'.

There was much wrangling about Wardell's right to private practice and his reputation never fully recovered after a prolonged inquiry into questionable conduct and poor workmanship on the Kew Asylum in the 1860s. Although he was cleared, he lost his official position with the government after drastic retrenchment in 1878. He built churches at Wangaratta, Geelong, Daylesford, Hamilton and Warrnambool.

A window on Wardell's bank showing the work of the stonemason at its best in reproducing the ogee curves and cusping of fifteenth-century Gothic

Another window detail on the same elevation showing the contrast between the depth of window and the combed ashlar wall surface

52

His secular work included the mansion Cliveden (1887), in Wellington Parade, which was demolished to make way for the Hilton Hotel, and some magnificent industrial architecture for the Williamstown dockyard. W.L. Vernon came to Australia in 1883 and was Wardell's partner from then until 1888.

Wardell's work has been compared with that of Edmund Blacket in New South Wales. According to Morton Herman 'he [Wardell] is the only considerable rival to Blacket in the field of Victorian ecclesiastical architecture in Australia, though most critics give Blacket pride of place'.[9] Not only was Blacket's secular architecture more extensive but, as he came to Australia sixteen years before Wardell, some of his work pre-dated Wardell's and must have had considerable influence. Most of his work was in New South Wales where, with his own sensitivity, he applied Decorated Gothic to churches and a *cottage orné* style to country vicarages and rectories. One can see the similarity between, say, the broach spire of St John's, Canberra (1878), and that of St John's, Toorak (1860-65); and his St John's Rectory at Bega (1850s) and Glenfern in East St Kilda (c.1857).

In Melbourne Blacket was disappointed with the buildings and the 'black stone and Portland Cement'. He said: 'The streets are very wide and quite straight, and you can see everywhere and I like the many open spaces planted with trees. The whole place is dreadfully *new*'.[10] Blacket designed Christ Church, Geelong (1847), and the Clarke Buildings for Trinity College in the Univer-

53

90 Queen Street (Safe Deposit Building, 1890), architect William Pitt, built by G.B. Leith. Compared with Wardell's bank next door, which is an essay in restraint, this is an example of the high Victorian Gothic restlessly overplayed

sity of Melbourne. Built in 1883, the latter show a fine blend of brickwork in English bond and sandstone dressings, and on the ground floor 'an arcaded cloister full of architectural mannerisms and mediocre details'.[11]

Men like Wardell and Blacket were prominent in the profession. There was also a wealth of English-trained architects perfectly competent in church design, coming as they did from a country rich in a Gothic heritage and finding their roots in a basically church-going community. It was not until the twentieth century that architects trained in Australia made a significant contribution.

A catalogue of churches would be tedious, but the following are selected. They cannot be regarded as typical except in so far as they all reflect the general characteristics of Gothic Revival. Each one is special, each one had a designer and each one is the product of creative thought worked out within the framework of Gothic grammar and a restricted budget. Mostly they were built within the third quarter of the last century.

George Reilly Cox designed St John's, Heidelberg (1849-51), with box pews similar to those at St James's Old Cathedral and still in perfect condition. As with most pre-gold rush buildings the technology was deficient and it had to be repaired four years later by Purchas and Swyer. The simple shape, the square tower and the setting of mature trees create a picture reminiscent of an English village church.

James Blackburn, jnr, designed St Mark's, Fitzroy (1855), a bluestone church

St John's Church of England, Heidelberg (1850). A stucco-covered brick building on a bluestone base in simple early Gothic style and reminiscent of the small English parish church. The shingles were replaced by slates in 1854. The nave is roofed with kingpost trusses

with a fine broach spire; Lloyd Tayler designed St Mary's, North Melbourne (1860), replacing an iron prefabricated church, but it was never completed to the size it was intended to be; and Charles Barrett designed Holy Trinity, Kew (1863), a bluestone church which, again, has a peculiarly English setting.

Dowden and Ross had been pupils of Pugin and designed St Mary's, West Melbourne (1872), and the original St Mary's, East St Kilda. Leonard Terry (Terry and Oakden) designed Holy Trinity, Williamstown (1872), thereby replacing an earlier iron prefabricated church with a building of bluestone with freestone dressings. It was to have been completed with a tower and spire, a landmark for ships in the bay, for Williamstown was a sea-conscious community, but shortage of funds prevented this completion.

In Richmond Arthur Newson and James Blackburn designed the original St Stephen's, Church Street. Commenced in 1849 and reputed to be the first bluestone church to be built outside the Melbourne town area, this was subsequently enlarged by Charles Webb and others. In South Yarra Webb designed Christ Church (begun 1858), the north aisle and spire being added by Reed, Henderson and Smart later in the century. This spire and others of this later stage (for example St Ignatius, Richmond) is a progression from the simple broach spire which belonged to the early stage of the style known as Decorated Gothic. They arise from behind a parapet with four pinnacles, rather like Lichfield Cathedral in

England. The pinnacles serve to channel any lateral thrust downwards through the corner buttresses of the tower.

Many architects well versed in Gothic design arrived in the mid-fifties. Ralph Wilson arrived in 1856 and practised under Crouch and Wilson. Nathaniel Billing had been a pupil of Gilbert Scott and emigrated to Port Fairy in 1853. There in Belfast, as it was called, he supervised the building of St Patrick's Church (1865), working from

drawings by Charles Hansom, the brother of the cab designer. He designed St John's Church in Belfast (1854-56) and Christ Church in Warrnambool (1860s). In Melbourne he was responsible for All Saints, St Kilda, and St Margaret's, Eltham. The latter church (1861) is a simple aisleless structure in brickwork, the original drawings for which reveal more diaper patterns in brickwork than were executed. It contains a walnut pulpit originally from St James's Old Cathedral. Billing came from the very source of Gothic Revival and 'his work was, like his character, distinguished by conscientious observance of correctness in detail'.[12]

St Margaret's was a forerunner of the great brick churches which, because of the greater variety and quality of bricks, became increasingly popular later in the century. In Brighton Evander McIver designed the Presbyterian Church in Wilson Street (1889, now St Cuthbert's Continuing) with rich textures of multicoloured brickwork; in Hawthorn Alfred Dunn designed Hawthorn Methodist Church (1888-89) where American Romanesque influences can be seen; and in Moonee Ponds A.E. Duguid designed the Wesleyan Church (1890, now Moonee Ponds Uniting) with a dominating slate-covered spire. For these and many more there was a good supply of interesting bricks—dark Hawthorns, pressed reds and creams from Northcote, and so on. We can see in this the influence of English architects like Butterfield and Street, and this leads on to a consideration of Reed and Barnes.

55

Holy Trinity Church of England, Coburg. The original church was built in 1849 and the present one in 1853-55. The walls are of local bluestone and the spire and dressings of imported sandstone. The architect is not known

Joseph Reed came to Melbourne among many immigrants in 1853 and rose to prominence by winning a competition for the Public Library (1853). The following year he was designing the Geelong Town Hall (1855) and thereafter came a steady succession of important buildings. His Wesley Church (1857-58) has already been referred to. He designed the Bank of New South Wales in Collins Street (1859), the facade of which has been removed to the grounds of the University, and the building for the Philosophical Institute of Victoria (later the Royal Society) at the junction of Victoria and La Trobe Streets (1859).[13]

Frederick Barnes became his partner in 1862 and one of their first jobs was to add the portico to John Gill's Collins Street Baptist Church. In the early 1860s Reed left the practice in the charge of Barnes and went overseas, where northern Italy inspired him with the beauty of brickwork in coloured patterns and shapes adding interest and texture to wall surfaces. After his return this treatment characterized many of his buildings, such as Ripponlea in Elsternwick (1868-87).

Reed and Barnes were responsible for Melbourne Town Hall, (1867-1928), Trades Hall in Lygon Street (1873), Presbyterian Ladies College in East Melbourne (1874, now demolished), Exhibition Building (1880) and ten banks. Some of these buildings will be described in Chapter 5. Reed and Barnes undertook extensive work for the University of Melbourne.

Their Wilson Hall, built in 1878 and burnt down in 1952, was described by

Sutherland as 'the most exquisite piece of architecture that the colony contains'.[14] Its Perpendicular Gothic windows and curved timber hammer-beam trusses with carved angels were much loved by generations of university students. Ormond College (1887), the second residential college to be established in the university, is a fine example of collegiate Gothic in Waurn Ponds sandstone and monumental in its massing. Queen's College, by Terry and Oakden, was

also commenced in the same year. This was faced with Fyansford sandstone. The Sugden Tower (1922-23) was designed by Eggleston and Oakley.

Of the twenty buildings for worship designed by Reed and Barnes, four will be referred to here. Their two most prominent city churches stand facing one another in Russell Street (corner of Collins Street). The Independent Church (1868) clearly shows the influence of Reed's tour of Lombardy. A Romanesque feeling and a rich tradition of brickwork are reflected in this building. The arch work in the arcading is a beautiful example of skilled bricklaying. Its great circular space is roofed over with a space frame. His Scots Church, built by David Mitchell in 1873, replaced Samuel Jackson's original building. It is built of two types of stone: from Waurn Ponds near Geelong and from Oamaru in New Zealand. Much of this has recently had to be replaced. Internally it is rich in timber furnishing.

English architects of that day were fostering the fashion for polychrome brickwork and Reed was considered to be its chief exponent here. This is evident, for instance, in St Jude's, Carlton (1866-70), where the patterned brickwork is quite charming with its multicolours and tuck-pointing. Reed intended a tower for this church, but money ran out and only a bellcote and porch were built. Internally the church is aisleless and roofed by an impressive series of curved cradles or waggon trusses. In 1890 Reed, Henderson and Smart designed the Memorial Chapel for the Convent of Mercy in Nicholson Street, Fitzroy, in Waurn

Independent Church (Uniting), corner Collins and Russell Streets (1867). Designed by Joseph Reed shortly after his return from Lombardy, this building is a triumph of nineteenth-century brick technology in patterned wall surfaces and finely worked arches. The interior is circular, roofed by trusses which together form a sort of space-frame

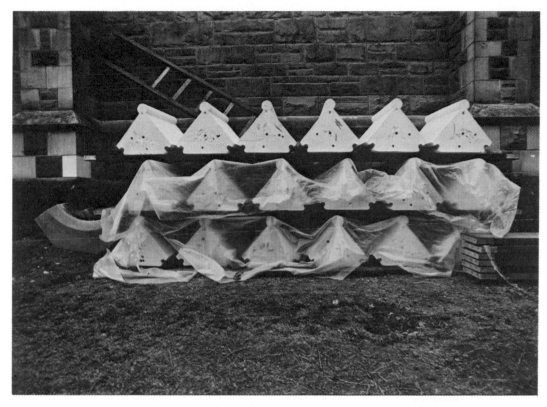

Ponds sandstone. Their work covered most religious denominations and ranged far over Victoria.

Reed, through a long and successful practice, was largely responsible for setting the visual pattern of Victorian Melbourne and, while doing so, was a source of strength to the profession. At the second attempt to found the Victorian Institute of Architects in 1872 Reed was its president, handing over to Redmond Barry two years later. He died in 1900. 'His work remains to mock the modern critic', said Robin Boyd in *The Australian Ugliness*, 'because it has a generosity and a scale which are proportionately beyond the capacity of today's enterprise'. (The name of Joseph Reed will be referred to from time to time in this book. It was linked with various partners throughout his professional life and this can cause confusion.)

Charles Webb was born at Sudbury, Suffolk, in 1821, the son of a bricklayer. In spite of a good education, he lacked the connections which in those days of patronage were vital to success. His brother James migrated to Melbourne in 1842 and sent for Charles, who weighed up his chances. He came to the conclusion that he had nothing to lose and joined his brother in Brighton as architect and surveyor and, even in competition with Charles Laing, soon became known as the colony's leading architect.

Like many young men of his day, he caught the gold fever of 1851 and joined the rush to the diggings. On his return he set up office in Collins Street for a three-year partnership with Thomas Taylor, and from then until 1890 there came a steady stream of the work basically of the two brothers. St Andrew's Church of England in Brighton (1857) with its high standard of bluestone masonry has not been entirely eclipsed by the monumental additions by Louis Williams in the 1950s. The Webb brothers were also responsible for the Church of Christ (1863) in Swanston Street and the first bluestone church in Melbourne proper—St Paul's Church of England on the corner of Swanston and Flinders Streets, the site of the old corn market. This was commenced in 1850 and was designed to seat 600 people. It had a square bluestone tower. The pews from this church can still be seen flanking the side aisles of the present cathedral. Webb's earlier buildings show brickwork which had to be protected with render as instanced in his Ebenezer Church in New Street, Brighton (1853-54), later

57

Methodist, now New Street Uniting. Twenty years later when Black Street Congregational (now Uniting) was built he used multicoloured brickwork. In 1876 he designed the John Knox Presbyterian Church on the corner of New Street and North Road. This church and the manse beside it are good examples of mid-Victorian Gothic Revival and the church has a broach spire interpreted in brickwork. This church replaced a smaller building by Lloyd Tayler. The original building of Melbourne Grammar School (1856), a bluestone version of collegiate Gothic, and Christ Church, South Yarra (1858), were also the work of Webb, in association with Thomas Taylor. He also designed Parliament Place (now incorrectly known as Tasma Terrace) in East Melbourne and Mac's Hotel in Franklin Street.

More than any other feature, the spire symbolized for Victorians the soaring, or 'aspiring', nature of Gothic, and was seen in an emotive or romantic role. Both of Melbourne's cathedrals have three spires each, two at the entrance end and the major one over the crossing. In each case they were redesigned to be taller and more impressive than those originally designed by the architect. The same thing happened to the spire of Wardell's St Ignatius', Richmond.

In the case of St Paul's, the Webb church lasted till 1880 when it was demolished to make way for the new cathedral. The English architect William Butterfield, whose work is seen at its best, or most typical, at Keble College Chapel, Oxford, had been

58

St Paul's Cathedral (1880-1931), designed by William Butterfield. This was the 'grandest of his sandstone interiors', but due to his resignation in 1886 (he never came to Australia), much of the detail can hardly be said to be his. The squared pattern of stones was a favourite decorative device of his. The spires were added in the 1930s. 'The inspiration of Siena is here.' This was 'Butterfield's final masterpiece'

commissioned to prepare plans in 1877 and the first drawings were done the following year. Butterfield never came to Australia and supervised the construction by correspondence in conjunction with the local architects, Terry and Oakden, an arrangement having in it the seeds of misunderstanding and failure. Frustration led to his resignation which took place two years before the cathedral was consecrated. His place was taken by F.J. Smart of Reed, Smart and Tappin, who supervised the work until the building was complete, except for the spires, as near as possible to Butterfield's original intentions, in January 1891.

Butterfield had commenced practice at a propitious time, for an unprecedented number of churches, church schools, parsonages and convents were to be built in England between the years 1840 and 1890. Churches were given more attention, and were illustrated and described in the building and architectural journals of the day increasingly through the century, and could make or break an architect's reputation. Of the best-known architects in the early years of the nineteenth century two out of three were church architects.

Butterfield, a high church Anglican, has been described as an 'uncomfortable genius'. 'How he hated taste', said John Summerson. 'It [Butterfield's ugliness] seems absolutely deliberate—even systematic: a calculated assault on the sensuous qualities latent in the simplest building forms . . . Is it possible, I wonder, to parallel this purposeful sadism in the whole history of architecture?'[15]

This refers, amongst other things, to the discords in his polychrome decoration and metallic tracery. He disliked the Rule of Taste and at St Paul's Cathedral he reveals internally what Lionel Brett described as his 'streaky bacon' style. The colour banding of the stone, Butterfield considered, would 'give life and the appearance of strength, and will make Melbourne Cathedral something special and interesting'. This however, is marvelloubly subdued and steadied by the floor of encaustic tile. The cathedral can be regarded as the culmination of Gothic Revival here, as much the centre of Melbourne as it is the centre of Anglicanism, and is worthy of praise.

He selected the stone from examples sent to England; Waurn Ponds, Pyrmont, and Barrabool. The banded stonework of the interior is superb, cream and grey, majestic and broad in detail. The roof is a fine dark brown local wood, and there are a few touches of soft red high up under the tower gallery. These are of plain tile, and the dado planned by Butterfield for the lower walls was to have been similarly restrained. The fussily patterned, green and orange tile dado actually executed is quite unsuitable, as indeed are most of the cathedral's fittings, but in spite of them Melbourne was Butterfield's final masterpiece.[16]

For parsonage or picturesque cottage Gothic was used here and there throughout the century, but with a restraint which characterizes Melbourne. The Hawthorns in Creswick Street, Hawthorn (1845), with its 2 feet (60 centimetres) thick bluestone walls squarely axed on the corners is one of the best domestic examples of bluestone masonry. The roof framing is blackwood and boxwood and the bargeboards are decorated with cusping suggestive of Gothic. At the rear a two-storey stable is separated from the house by a walled-in courtyard, a reminder that in those days the land beyond the river was wild and unsettled.

Dating from the 1850s, we have 3 Elm Grove, Richmond Hill, which is mildly Gothic in early brickwork because of its connection with St Ignatius' Church. Roseneath in Pakington Street, Kew (1856), has kauri floors and sits unobtrusively behind a three-storey block of flats in what remains of its garden laid out by Von Mueller. Glenfern (1857), on the corner of Inkerman and Hotham Streets, East St Kilda, has Gothic arches and angled chimneys. Ivy Grange in Malmsbury Street, Kew (1864), has a tower built in cream brick which contrasts with the dark bluestone.

These are picked at random out of many examples. Towards the end of the century we have 1 Sorrett Avenue, Malvern (1890), which is another stone house having a deep-set arch under the gable and picturesque chimneys. In Brighton, 38 Black Street (1889-90) is the only work in Victoria, so far as is known, by the architect Horbury Hunt, whose churches are so well known in New South Wales. The curved window ar-

59

ches, stained glass and large brick chimneys give this house a cosy Gothic flavour.

The above are included in this chapter because they have features traditionally associated with church building. Gothic was generally accepted as the way to design a church, but the style permeated the culture of the age and affected the furniture, the bandstands and the drinking fountains of those days for the same reason that we like to recapture a beautiful past in our 'modern' houses, hotels and restaurants— an incorrigible nostalgia. So students of architecture learned their Gothic construction and details to serve a church-going public, and when it was announced to the Institute that *Paley's Gothic Mouldings* was out of print it was something of a disaster, because in the 1890s it was as essential a textbook as Banister Fletcher's *History of Architecture*.[17] Gothic Revival continued into the twentieth century with such buildings as Nahum Barnet's Church of England Chinese Mission, 119-125 Little Bourke Street (1902), and later merged with American Gothic and mannerist influences, slowly losing touch with the essence of Gothic structure and finally dying out with the outbreak of the Second World War.

In a colourless middle-class environment we envy the romanticism and imagination of the Victorians. Granted all the prudery, piety and double standards of the age, Melbourne, a very 'special' city because of all this background, would have been the poorer without those architects capable of accepting conventional stylism and applying it with skill and originality.

A house in Parliament Place (1890) showing Gothic features in its stucco facing and cast iron railing and valence work. It was designed by J.A.B. Koch as the Manse for the Lutheran Trinity Church

60

Above: A unique house in Queens Road, South Melbourne, dating from the 1880s, with corbelled brick quoins, decorated barge boards and Tudor chimneys

61

Left: 157 Hotham Street, East Melbourne, This house, which was standing in 1859 and added to in 1866, is a combination of bluestone structure and decorative timberwork with a Gothic Revival touch. The unusual sweep of the gables adds to its delightfully picturesque character. It was the home of Clement Hodgkinson, Deputy Surveyor-General. The architect may have been Joseph Reed

There is no doubt Melbourne had convicts as cheap labour. There is a gallery for them in St James's Old Cathedral; convicts built the defence works at Gellibrand, worked on other buildings at Williamstown and laid the bluestone for Sydney Road. But Melbourne had the great advantage over Sydney in not having to struggle as a penal settlement. In 1848 the *Randolph*, with a consignment of rehabilitated convicts on board, was sent on its way from Melbourne, as a result of local agitation, to Port Jackson and from there to Moreton Bay. Free settlers came in increasing numbers and the town soon outstripped Sydney, with a steady growth.

Melbourne, more than any other city, was considered to be the metropolis of the southern hemisphere. It was here that the trade, business and pleasure of Australia chiefly centred, and Melbourne became the source and headquarters of much Australian commerce.

> The Melbourne man is always on the lookout for business, the Sydney man waits for business to come to him. The one is always in a hurry, the other takes life more easily. And as it is with business, so it is with pleasure.[1]

There was more 'society' in Melbourne—balls, parties and intellectual life; for entertainment there were theatrical and musical performances, racing, cricket, football and athletic clubs. The bushman or squatter who came to town to 'knock down his cheque' was attracted by the vitality of the place, with its 1120 pubs in which drink was

Chapter 5

Late Victorian Melbourne

I love art, and I love history; but it is living art and living history I love. If we have no hope for the future, I do not see how we can look back on the past with pleasure.
William Morris

plentiful but comfort hard to come by.

The history of Australia is the history of her cities. Although the inland towns of Victoria grew during the gold rush and the percentage of Victorians living in Melbourne declined, this trend was soon reversed. With the decline of alluvial gold-mining, a steady stream of diggers and casual fortune-seekers returned to city life. In 1871 the six capital cities contained one-quarter of the population and by 1901 one-

third. The function of Melbourne in Victoria became as a commercial centre linking the hinterland to world markets.

According to the census of 1857, Melbourne proper had 36 988 people, exclusive of Chinese, living in 4196 houses of brick or stone and 3476 of wood or iron. By 1870 the population had risen to 207 000, by 1880 to 281 000 and by 1890 to 500 000.

Redmond Barry appealed for beauty and elegance in Melbourne's buildings. Steady immigration brought architects to the colony and the Melbourne Directory for 1888 listed 250 practising architects, 680 builders and contractors, 41 quarries, 120 brick and tile makers and 120 timber merchants, which gives us an idea of the building activity at the height of the boom. In that year Anthony Trollope visited Melbourne and described it as a magnificent city that was 'undoubtedly not only the capital of Victoria but also of Australia'. He was impressed by the width of the streets and the allocation of large areas within the city to public gardens. He added: 'Boastfulness I found everywhere but nowhere louder or more assertive than in Melbourne'.[2]

Such was the economic growth that by 1887 annual imports and exports for Victoria amounted to £110 million ($220 million) and during the four years 1886-90 more than £20 million ($40 million) was borrowed for public works. In this period Victoria imported £54 million ($108 million) worth more goods than she exported.

The 1880s was a decade of unprecedented irresponsibility during which no less than £30 million ($60 million) was raised in London loans. As Michael Cannon puts it:

£9 million of this had to be applied to paying off earlier loans. The public debt increased from £22 million to £46 million in Victoria alone. Coupled with private borrowing, about £60 million in loan money flowed into Victoria during the boom years. In one year, 1888, when Victoria's population reached one million, the circulation of money in Melbourne increased by 84 per cent.[3]

This was artificial and, as it turned out, temporary prosperity. The government spent much of this money on ill-conceived extensions to the railway system, squandering it on wasted or useless lines. It was a free enterprise laissez-faire system, but the Victorian Parliament lost credibility through the enterprises of its members who were, of course, capitalists. To be fair, the parliamentarian of those days had no salary for his job and was therefore frequently on the lookout for a profitable piece of real estate. Many of them promoted worthless development companies and built themselves gorgeous mansions, thus fostering a general atmosphere of optimism and affluence. In the 1890s it was not only their careers which ended in ignominy and suicide but the bulk of the suffering was borne by the general public who had invested in their schemes.

Land prices rose sharply at the height of the boom and the Saturday issue of one morning newspaper would carry 170 columns of land-sale advertisements. There were many visitors to the city who recorded their impressions. One of them, Mark Twain, said of these vigorous times:

Melbourne spreads around over an immense area of ground. It is a stately city architecturally as well as in magnitude. It has an elaborate system of cable-car services, it has museums, and colleges, and schools, and public gardens, and electricity and gas, and libraries, and theatres, and mining centres, and wool centres, and centres for the arts and sciences; and boards of trade, and ships, and railroads, and a harbour, and social clubs, and racing clubs, and a squatter club sumptuously housed and appointed, and as many churches and banks as can make a living. In a word, it is equipped with everything that goes to make the modern great city.[4]

That was the contemporary account of an eye-witness. Geoffrey Serle sums it up in the light of history:

Victoria had been supplying one-third of the world's gold production and about one-sixth of Britain's vast imports of wool; her scale of business activity was twice as great as New South Wales... A sense of modernity, of being in the van of progress, tinged the Victorian outlook... Public buildings were erected on a grand extravagant scale, while the banks and mercantile houses vied with each other in building imposing palaces, fronted with ornate cornices, columns and capitals; but here and there a crazy corrugated iron or weatherboard shanty remained in the centre of the city... The streets were well flagged, kerbed and channelled, with iron foot-bridges across the deep gutters.[5]

More than any other, the Exhibition Building (1880) seems to sum up this age of affluence and optimism. Ever since the 1851 Great Exhibition in London there had been minor attempts at emulation in Australia (for example the Exhibition Building erected on the site of the old Royal Mint in William Street in 1854, which apparently decayed in 1868), but nothing on the scale of the two great Melbourne exhibitions of 1880 and 1888. Parliament voted £100 000 ($200 000) for the building and a site was chosen in Carlton. The Reed and Barnes building is uninhibited, makes its point magnificently and exudes the confidence of the times. At the time of construction it was the largest structure in Australasia and is still one of the largest places for public assembly in the country. No doubt the Sydney Exhibition of 1879 provided the incentive for competition.

A brick-built stucco-covered structure, it has a main east-west hall with timber trusses and galleries and, over the point of intersection with the transept, a dome constructed on a brick drum and pendentives of a sort. This dome is octagonal in plan (and therefore not a true dome) and slightly pointed, or Gothic, in shape. In this Reed may well have been influenced by Brunelleschi's great dome over Florence Cathedral. The drawings were superbly done by Frederick Barnes and the builder was David Mitchell.

Ornamental stucco work was expressive of this age and can be seen on parapets, copings, urns, finials, cartouches and date plaques. Sometimes it was cheaply mass-produced and sometimes skilfully worked by the plasterer. At the Exhibition Building the large fountain in the gardens is an example of decorative stucco work, seen at its best at night in changing coloured lights. The building was finished with a George Fincham pipe organ, another feature expressive of the full-throated opulence of the day.

The building was filled with the products and inventions of the Victorian age. Complete railway engines and carriages were exhibited and people could see typewriters, gas stoves, lawnmowers, ice-chests, and elaborate bathroom and toilet fittings. Nor was culture overlooked. Two concerts daily were heard and

eventually half a million people attended these concerts. An operatic company performed portions of the latest Wagnerian opera. There was another great collection of art and sculpture. Visitors, surfeited with culture, or tired of walking down the endless aisles that were packed with commercial exhibits, could visit the largest aquarium in Australia, or take the new lift into the dome of the Exhibition Building, and from there view the panorama of Melbourne spread out below.[6]

64

Exhibition Building, Carlton (1879-80), architects Reed and Barnes. Designed to house the International Exhibition of 1880, this building is dominated by a huge octagonal dome rising from brick pendentives. The building is finished in plaster but is structurally of brick and timber. Fitted with Fincham's massive pipe organ, the building epitomized Melbourne's optimism and ascendency in an expanding economy

*Oberwyl, 33 Burnett Street, St Kilda (1856). A
delicate example of Greek Revival detailing in timber
and plaster*

*(Detail) This photograph shows some of the Greek
decorative details in this building*

In the houses of the period can be seen a steady growth of affluence and a rise in the standard of living. This can be illustrated in an area like Brighton. The homes of the mid-century, like Chilton in Wellington Street (c.1857), Tynefield in Tynefield Court (1860) and Seagrove in Middle Crescent (1873) were simple and colonial with twelve-light, double-hung sash windows beneath verandah roofs. Then in the 1870s the tower appeared; quite possibly its

Farleigh, 6 Farleigh Court, Brighton (1865), architect Charles Webb. A stucco-faced house with dignified classical proportions. Weston Bate writes that 'A watercolour of Farleigh, probably painted in the nineties, shows the park-like atmosphere which was aimed at'

Government House (1872-76), architect William Wardell. A stately mansion reminiscent of Queen Victoria's Osborne House. This picture shows the north elevation with its faithful reproduction of Renaissance detail in stucco on brickwork. Like Treasury Building in Spring Street, this is a loggia treatment with a pavilion at either end

popularity was promoted by J.J. Clark and Peter Kerr's design for Government House (1872). In this great mansion there is a definite resemblance to Queen Victoria's Osborne House on the Isle of Wight, which had two towers. Government House tower stands in a commanding position amid choice landscaping and rises to 144 feet (44 metres). And so a tower came to be regarded as a status symbol among the affluent.

Round the bayside we find towers built on the north side of the street with a view towards the bay, and it has been suggested, but hardly seriously, that the Russian invasion scare had something to do with this. Thus in Brighton, Chilton in Wellington Street, Bronte, 2 Sussex Street and Grutli, 57 Halifax Street (1880s) all have towers. Billila in Halifax Street (begun 1876) has a later tower showing Art Nouveau decorative details. There are many others. Maritimo (1885, but now demolished) in Williamstown looked out over the shipping. Between 1872 and 1874 Lloyd Tayler designed three great Brighton houses, all with towers: Chevy Chase, Blair Athol and Kamesburgh. A tower was added to Como in South Yarra at this time.

Arcaded verandahs took over from the simple post-and-beam style and coloured leadlights filled the fanlights over the front doors. The twelve-light, double-hung colonial window gave way to the taller window glazed with larger panes of Chance's sheet glass and coarser sash frames and mouldings, the stiles of the upper sash finishing with horns beyond the mortice and tenon joint.

69

Marema, 161 Church Street, Brighton (1887). Built by Alfred Harston on a bluestone substructure with walls of dark Hawthorns and lighter string courses and arches. This is one of the tower houses of Brighton

70

*Blair Athol, Leslie Grove, Brighton (1872), architect
Lloyd Tayler. A house with mild Gothic Revival
characteristics. Built before piped water in Brighton,
it has three wells at the rear whence water was hand-
pumped to a tank over the servants' quarters*

St John of God Hospital, 29 Heathfield Road, Brighton (1881). One of the great tower houses of Brighton with a two-storey verandah

72

Maritimo, The Strand, Williamstown (1885). Built for William Henry Croker, a well-known solicitor with a big practice in maritime law, it was sold to S.G. Garnsworthy, whose father built the nearby White House, in 1922. Now demolished, Maritimo had a tower with built-in seats and a fine view of the bay. There was a high standard of brickwork and a touch of Gothic in the arched openings. The glazing in the verandah was added later

Chevy Chase, 203 Were Street, Brighton (1881). A great tower house almost identical to St John of God Hospital. Both were built by Andrew Thompson

74

*Kamesburgh (Anzac Hostel), 103 North Road,
Brighton (1874, extended 1884), architect Lloyd
Tayler. A forty-room mansion and, according to
Weston Bate, 'one of Brighton's marvels on ten acres
of land, two acres of which were fine gardens kept
by William Kenner'*

Ellesmere House, 80 Princess Street, Kew. One of the gracious homes of Kew of the 1880s, having a remarkable dome-light over the intersection of corridors and a timber verandah valence

The slate-covered roof, often framed in an M shape and hipped back at the ends, was hidden from view behind an ornate parapet decorated with statuettes and urns. Turrets and domes on more prominent buildings would be framed up in angle iron and roofed with slate cut to the curve or pressed zinc sheeting. Internal finishings were lavish and ceilings presented an opportunity for the plasterer's craft. Cornices were broad and heavily moulded and the centre of the ceiling, where the gas light was suspended, was marked by an acanthus leaf (or even Australian flora) rosette. To make this required much skill by plasterers, in the tradition of British craftsmen who created their finest ceilings in the days of the Stuarts and early Hanoverians. Sometimes the rosette was pre-formed of plaster, cannabic composition, papier maché, brass or cast iron. The more elaborate way was to produce a deep wax mould in situ immediately below the ceiling, the wet plaster being poured in from above. The final operation was the removal of the wax mould by slow heat. Architraves and skirtings were expansive and richly moulded. Verandahs and porches were paved with stone, marble or encaustic tile from Mintons in England.

On many a site the remains of an earlier home can be seen with the remodelled home of the later, affluent, period creating a new facade. Those who had made their fortunes wished to display their wealth, and in most cases the earlier structure breathed a simple colonial atmosphere and the later addition an ostentatious Italianate one. The latter relied heavily on imports of labour and materials.

For instance, the additions to the simple home called St George's in Toorak were drastic. This was an elegant example of a quiet classical style, slightly French in feeling, attuned to a spacious, almost woodland setting, but the front of the house was completely remodelled in the grand style by Joseph Clark in 1877. (This became Mandeville Hall, now Loreto Convent.) The furnishings, executed by Gillows of London, cost about £170 000 ($340 000) and the

workmen brought out from England took twenty months to carry out the job. Italian workmen were imported to lay the marble halls.

Broughton Hall, formerly Tara, in Berwick Street, Camberwell, was also an 1880 development from an earlier building dating from 1859. Here John O'Shannassy built a home which expressed his affluence and position in life. In the entrance hall he incorporated plaster bas-reliefs of Ghiberti's

Illawarra, Illawarra Crescent, Toorak (1890-91), built for Charles Henry James, a 'land boomer'. Illawarra is now owned by the National Trust and contains cast iron ornamentation of unique pattern and of world-wide importance

Mandeville Hall (now Loreto Convent), Toorak (1877). An early example of the opulent 'boom' style mansion often, as in this case, enclosing an earlier simpler home. All the features of the Italianate style are here — the 'orders' of architecture, the arcaded loggias, the roof parapets and the costly furnishings and finishes (architect Charles Webb)

twelve panels from the Baptistry doors at Florence and the soffite of the staircase was of inlaid wood. O'Shannassy was not only Premier of Victoria but a shrewd land dealer. He was responsible for routing the railway line through Camberwell in its present position, crossing Burke Road, as it did, with a level crossing. Before the cutting went through in the 1920s this part of the Box Hill line was a very steep gradient for steam trains.

Malvern House, part of Caulfield Church of England Grammar School, was designed as a mansion by Thomas Watts and Son in 1891. Both it and Broughton Hall reveal in stucco a Palladian treatment of pilasters and pediments to accentuate the windows. In the Malvern building the central entrance leads into a huge top-lit two-storeyed hall ringed at first floor level by cantilevered balconies giving access to the bedrooms. In this and in many other homes of the period the grand open staircase is derived from Jacobean houses.

Stonnington, 336 Glenferrie Road, Malvern, now the State College of Victoria, has been used as a vice-regal residence and was designed by Charles D'Ebro in 1892, having elaborate loggias and cornices and all the extravagances of the period. It was built on the fortunes of Cobb and Co. At Sunbury, then far distant from Melbourne, where the Jackson brothers had settled forty years earlier, Rupertswood was designed by George Browne in 1874 for William Clarke. In this grand house the great rooms of extravagant dimensions are shaded by verandahs and the sun penetrates through

the filter of cast iron lacework. The whole scheme is enhanced by the setting, the landscaping and by Jackson's Creek. George Browne also designed a Gothic memorial to Clarke in the Melbourne General Cemetery.

At Werribee Thomas and Andrew Chirnside bought land from J.H. Wedge, the surveyor who had been associated with Batman, who in turn had bought the land in the 'treaty' with the natives. The property was a neighbour to Staughton's Exford,

referred to in Chapter 2. The Chirnsides commissioned James Henry Fox, quantity surveyor to the Victorian Government, to design a mansion. Chirnside (Werribee Park) was consequently built between 1874 and 1877 to a grand design in one contract (except for the outbuildings which are earlier). This building, with its expression of dominance, was a far cry from the simple ground-hugging colonial homestead, as the Roman Doric order is expressed in Waurn

48 Burnett Street, St Kilda (1877), a fine example of affluent building in Melbourne. Interesting features include alternating triangular and curved pediments over the windows and 'dummy' windows where the strictly Renaissance wall treatment requires them. The house has been recently renovated

77

The Willows, St Kilda Road, an example of the type of gracious home which used to be here before St Kilda Road was zoned commercial. It was originally called Estella and was built in 1890 for James Downie. The huge ballroom has been demolished

Ponds sandstone in the grand manner. The interior has recently been restored according to conservative restoration principles and the original surfaces, where possible, preserved. The lake, the grotto, the lawns and the planting combine to make an interesting example of nineteenth-century landscaping along the banks of the Werribee River. The Catholic Church used Werribee Park as a theological college and made many alterations and additions.

Labassa in Manor Grove, Caulfield North (1890), was designed by J.A.B. Koch and is another example of where Italian workmen were imported to work on a specific building. The Corinthian columns are of cast iron coloured to imitate red marble. The balustrades were originally surmounted with animal sculptures and urns and the elaborate brackets and chimneys are finished with stucco cornices.

Anketell Henderson built Myoora, 405

Alma Road, North Caulfield, in 1886-87. This is a very substantial house with a dominating tower and bold classical, or Renaissance, detailing internally and externally.

Ravenswood in York Avenue, Heidelberg (1890), reflected the Italianate era with its magnificent arcaded verandahs and became a centre for parties, concerts and dances. It had the same atmosphere of cultured magnificence as John Wilkinson's Ross

79

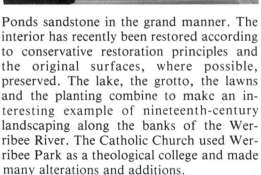

Chirnside (Werribee Park) 1874-77, designed by James Henry Fox in the grand manner. The design is Roman Renaissance to the last detail. The tower and loggia are expressive of the power and the dominance of the pastoral industry which was the mainstay of Victoria's prosperity

Labassa, 2 Manor Grove, Caulfield North (1890). This is a good example of the Italianate style. Italian craftsmen were imported to work on this house. The recessed panels are of pink marble, and the columns, though pink, are of cast iron. The verandah has vaulted construction at the first floor ceiling level and the internal finishes are sumptuous

Swinton, Swinton Avenue, Kew (1858-59), architect unknown. Built of Hawthorn bricks and rendered, this is one of the houses sited to command a view over the Yarra valley, but this one has extra charm and delicacy in the tower and eaves detailing. Inside there is an octagonal room

House, Cotham Road, Kew (architect H. Shalles, 1889), and Merridale in Sackville Street (architect John Mickelburgh, the elder, 1884). Berrington (1880s) and La Vernia (1889) in the same street are likewise magnificent. The garden of La Vernia is another interesting example of nineteenth-century landscaping, with a perimeter walk snaking in and out of shrubbery. Some, like Edward Latham's Raheen in Studley Park Road, had the same Italianate features interpreted in brickwork. Built in 1870, Raheen has a fine view over the Yarra valley with classical terracing going down the slope. From it 'the northern suburbs lie stretched below upon a variegated carpet which stretches from the Dandenong Ranges to Mount Macedon'.[7]

The house which visually has the closest links with the English Regency tradition is Trawalla, 22 Lascelles Avenue, Toorak. Built in 1867, this building has a symmetrical west elevation dominated by a fine bow. The composition is articulated by a two-storey verandah of elegance and generosity. Following the depression years of the 1930s and subsequent decay, this building has been renovated.

Rippon Lea in Elsternwick, designed by Reed and Barnes, developed into a thirty-three-room mansion by 1887. Described as Frederick Thomas Sargood's 'Xanadu', it is remarkable for its Lombardic feeling expressed in the arches and polychrome brickwork. A similar feeling can be found in the Independent Church in Collins Street, by the same architects, and neither can be described as Australian. It is another exam-

80

Trawalla, 22 Lascelles Avenue, Toorak (1867). More than any other, this building reflects the simple gracious curves of Regency architecture

81

*Rippon Lea, Hotham Street, Elsternwick (1863-87).
Designed by Reed and Barnes, this great house was
the immediate result of Reed's tour of Northern Italy
and incorporated brickwork in coloured patterns and
round-headed arches. The house with its porte-cochère
and fernery and the landscaping in one great design
express the ultimate in Melbourne's nineteenth-century
mansions*

82

*(Details) The details of this house show clearly some
of the trade skills available at that time in
bricklaying, stone masonry, joinery, metalwork; and
the significance of sculpture to the Victorian mind*

ple of the rich mixture of overseas influences which until now had been a vital part of a vigorous community. Rippon Lea with its *porte-cochère*, its conservatory and, above all, its gardens, probably by William Guilfoyle, is permeated by the atmosphere of late-Victorian affluence. Incidentally, in the gardens there is an example of a 1930s swimming-pool with its ancillary buildings.

Lowther Hall, 17 Leslie Road, Essendon, was designed by Lawson and Grey in 1890 for Coiler McCracken. It is a magnificent example of the use of the grand Corinthian order, making a decisive monumental statement for a two-storeyed house. According to the practice of the day, coins of the realm and current newspapers were deposited behind the foundation stone.[8]

In the world scene this was the age of unbounded optimism in engineering, and worldwide achievements had their repercussions in the colonies. The 'tyranny of distance' was softening with the age of steam, and Isambard Brunel's screw-driven iron ship S.S. *Great Britain* made a total of twenty-seven runs to Australia. The construction of the Eiffel Tower in 1888 was much in the news and the Forth Bridge was under construction the following year. Over the Thames, Tower Bridge with its mighty bascules was completed in the early eighties. The great open spaces of Australia were being defined by Lysaght's fencing wire and from the point of view of technological achievement Melbourne was not far behind Europe or America.

83

Its cable tram system was

known all over the world for its completeness and for the general excellence of its management... Rapidly, yet steadily, and almost gracefully, the dummy and car glide along the rails moved by an unseen force... without undue noise or undue danger. If a would-be passenger misses one car he knows that he will not have to wait more than a minute or so for the next.[9]

One or two engine houses remain. One is situated on the corner of Nicholson and Gertrude Streets, Fitzroy, and another on the corner of Bridge Road and Hoddle Street, Richmond. The Fitzroy building, having a system of steel trusses supported by cast iron columns, is grand and functional internally but fussily overplayed externally. (This seems to have been the besetting fault of Victorian architecture.) It was designed to house the two engines, pulleys and driving drums made by Shanks of Arbroath. The engineering was impressive rather than sophisticated, especially the driving drums 12 feet (3.6 metres) in diameter, with grooved peripheries lined with wood, 'which arrangement in combination with the tension apparatus, secures sufficient adhesion to haul 24 000' [over 7 kilometres] of cable heavily loaded'.[10]

Bridge building had by now passed beyond the stage of stone arches; the second Prince's Bridge, designed by J.H. Grainger, had its foundation stone laid in 1886. Lacking the artless charm of Lennox's arch, the bridge was built for the traffic age. On a base of Harcourt granite nearly 1000 tons of wrought iron and 200 tons of cast iron span the Yarra in three great arches.

Invention and technology stimulated building. The hydraulic lift was making high-rise buildings feasible, but the increased height of these buildings outstripped the limitations of fire safety. Iron girders over 3 feet (1 metre) deep were being imported and iron was extensively used for roof trusses. In 1889 the raw sugar store at the Yarraville Refinery was roofed by a 100-foot (30 metre) truss of steel and timber. The tie beam had a scarved joint at the centre secured by two fish-plates and fourteen bolts.[11]

Yet it was technology that architects were strangely reluctant to exploit, choosing instead the security of academic discussion on styles and philosophies. For instance, Kirkpatrick, a Sydney architect, produced and published two possible elevations for the same house, one Jacobean and the other French Renaissance, and in Melbourne Cyril Blacket gave a lecture entitled 'Materials appropriate to various styles of architecture'. This was typical of nineteenth-century architects. John Nash of London, years earlier, had his office divided into two parts, one for classic and one for Gothic. Now Wilson Dobbs in Australia was pleading for a truly Australian architecture.

Because of this emphasis on elevational treatment we should expect to see a variety of styles in the buildings of this period. The multi-storey commercial buildings now breaking the skyline were clothed with the dress fashionable at the time or desired by the owner, very much as the people in the street were clothed according to fashion or 'taste'. The external load-bearing walls, sometimes as much as 3 feet (1 metre) thick at the base, were brickwork, which meant that a stone facing on the front facade could easily be block-bonded in. Internally there were iron stanchions and steel or iron beams. The cavity wall was known at least as early as 1879.[12]

Melbourne has some unique public buildings. Perhaps Parliament House is the most noticeable. It occupies a pivotal position and needs to be set off by a square or public space in front of it. It was built in stages between 1856 and 1890 to the designs of Peter Kerr and John George Knight. The basement and plinth are bluestone and the remainder is stone from Mount Difficult in the Grampians and from Darley (Bacchus Marsh). Knight was an authority on building stones and was described in his day as 'a very nice fellow, a real gentleman, and a jolly old chap'. He was respected for his commonsense and resource.[13]

Peter Kerr had been associated with Charles Barry in London; and Barry had designed the Reform Club in London in 1837. The latter's influence can be felt in the great portico which extends across the front of the building. Real gold leaf was used in the interior decoration, and the floors were laid in encaustic tile. The library with its curving staircase, then Queen's Hall and finally the great west portico and entrance steps were completed successively. The building was to have been surmounted by a

Parliament House, Spring Street (1856-92), architects Peter Kerr and J.C. Knight. Built of Stawell stone on a bluestone substructure, this is a magnificent example of the Roman Doric order incorporated into a giant portico as a tour de force closing the vista up Bourke Street. This photograph shows the incredible richness of the entrance portico in materials and trade skills

dome, but this was never built. Nor was the north wing built, making this one of the unfinished buildings of Melbourne.

The huge Roman Doric portico makes its point as a grand termination to Bourke Street (except for the spires of St Patrick's Cathedral silhouetted above it), while the interior sequence of spaces culminating in the Legislative Council Chamber is a scholarly application of Palladian principles. It is described by Sutherland as 'the stateliest building in Melbourne',[14] and without doubt it is the ultimate expression in a public building of the affluence of nineteenth century Melbourne. Parliament House

> was the grandest in the Empire outside Westminster, and the Catholic Cathedral the largest in the southern hemisphere. Government House was larger than the Viceroy of India's or the Lord Lieutenant of Dublin's, and its ballroom was larger than Buckingham Palace's.[15]

The Law Courts in William Street (1877-84) were designed by Smith and Johnson. They were influenced by the Four Courts in Dublin, a picture of which hung in the architects' office and is now in the library foyer of the Courts. In a complicated sequence of spaces the dominating area under the dome is the circular library and galleries around it. A cobbled courtyard contains a carriage entrance with gas lamps and balustrading, and deep balconies are a feature of the street elevations. The courts themselves are marvellously fitted

with joinery and the dome over this building with a peristyle round its drum is more truly Roman, or Renaissance, than that of the Exhibition Building. The building construction and detailing are impressive, from the bluestone staircases to the inner brick dome. The outer dome is fabricated with great skill out of wrought iron angle. Before the days of high-rise Melbourne it was these two domes and the tower of Government House that

dominated the skyline when the city was viewed from arriving or departing ships.

The model of classical, or Renaissance, architecture is the Elizabeth Street Post Office, (begun 1867), also by Smith and Johnson. Its significance lies in its application of three 'orders of architecture' superimposed one over the other on the pattern of the Colosseum: Doric at ground level, Ionic at first floor and Corinthian above. By the end of 1867 only two of these storeys had been built owing to exceptional difficulties in the foundations. (The site was the old creek bed running down Elizabeth Street and in recent years during excavation for new buildings old foot bridges across the creek have been discovered.) The third storey and clock tower were finally added in the eighties. Of all Melbourne's Victorian buildings none shows Renaissance detailing in stonework with such scholarship and finesse as this. The components in the elevation fit together like a Latin prose composition.

In the eighties also, the Town Hall was finally completed with a magnificent portico which straddles the footpath with a dramatic third dimension, thus saving the building from being a flat facade.

Another classical feature was the giant 'order' used externally, and this also seemed to fit the expansive spirit of the times. Two buildings show this with Corinthian porticos: the State Library in Swanston Street (begun 1853) and the Trades Hall in Lygon Street (1873), both by Reed and Barnes. Architects handled these porticos with a competence springing from their profes-

86

Supreme Court, William Street (commenced 1874), architects Smith and Johnson. View of dome from carriage entrance. This is a thoroughly Renassance building, pieced together with classical correctness and dominated by the dome

sional training. The first is in natural stone and the second is in stucco and both face west, which means that the afternoon light brings out the best in classical mouldings, column flutings and details.

From the time Serlio's and Palladio's writings were translated into English every architect and man of taste considered it part of his education to know the orders of architecture and the basic rules for classical proportion. In fact the word 'taste' was unknown until the Renaissance. In the search for harmony in plan and elevation, each building was subjected to this intellectual discipline. Each part of it—wall, column, pilaster, pier, arch and lintel—had its exact dimensions and place. The result was a highly self-conscious art and to this intellectual discipline every architect, by his very training, submitted himself.

Ideas and styles flowed freely in those heady days. William Pitt, a one-time member of Parliament, typified the colourful characters in the architectural profession. Born in 1855, he commenced a practice in 1879 which, coinciding partly with the boom years, proved prolific. Of Pitt's many theatres the most festive was the Princess, built in 1887, Queen Victoria's jubilee year, and in some way symbolic of this decade when Melbourne reached the heights of achievement and culture. The theatre was an imaginitive building for a theatre-loving people, its facade and furnishings rich in allegorical figures symbolizing the arts. Its roof would slide open to the night air.

More exotic still was Rickard's Opera

87

The Post Office, Elizabeth Street (1859-89), designed by A.E. Johnson. This photograph shows one bay of the lower set of superimposed 'orders' of architecture, that is, the Roman Doric, an exercise in simple classical geometry and masonry skills fast dying out

House, also in Exhibition Street, built around the turn of the century. Renamed the Tivoli Theatre in 1915, this building had an elevation with Moorish arches. It was demolished in 1970.

Pitt's best-known office buildings are the Olderfleet and the Rialto (475 and 497 Collins Street respectively). Being near the original port, this is where firms connected with customs, freight and shipping had their offices. The Olderfleet (1889-90) is a highly decorated Gothic fantasy with marble columns, pointed arches and coloured mosaics round windows and main entrance. It had hydraulic lifts. The Rialto, of the same date, has a remarkable side elevation with multi-storey verandahs. Internally it has ornamental stamped zinc work and metal lathing for its ceilings. It is significantly in advance of the Olderfleet from the point of view of fire-resistance. 'Cinder concrete', a lightweight aggregate. probably waste from glass smelters, was used over the vaulted corrugated ceilings, and each bay was designed to have full-height solid brick walls. Stone stairs were built into fire-proof walls of solid brick. Fire doors were held

Ercildoune, 66 Napier Street, Footscray (1876). This building was built as a branch of the National Bank and is an impressive classical elevation on a bluestone base. The simple architraves, string course and eaves cornice give it a rare civic dignity

Lalor House, Richmond (1888), designed by W. Wolf of Edinburgh Street, Richmond, for Dr Joseph Lalor, Health Inspector for Richmond. The Corinthian order of architecture and arched loggia treatment are Italian and the floors of the balcony and verandah are of black marble tiles. The mantles also are marble

open with fusible links, and within a year of this building the first exposed ceiling-hung sprinkler system appeared in Melbourne. At the time of writing the front part of the Olderfleet and the whole of the Rialto are preserved. Between them the Winfield Building by Speight and D'Ebro stands defiant of modern high-rise Melbourne.

G.S. Coppin's model tenement (Gordon House) in Little Bourke Street was designed by Pitt in 1883, showing a light touch of Gothic which was usual for a building designed for charitable purposes. Built of strong clean elements, basalt, brickwork and timber, this building has been imaginitively recycled. A person seated in the courtyard beside a Canary Island palm can experience light and space surrounded by balconies, jasmine and strolling people at three levels above. This is an exciting multi-purpose structure (such as the Rialto could become) and a cool haven on a hot day.

Many other buildings came from this prolific designer. First, in the city, there were the Stock Exchange in Collins Street and Queen Street (an L-shaped block around Wardell's ANZ Bank, 1888-89); Leitrim Hotel, 128 Little Lonsdale Street (1888); and Markillie's Hotel, 562 Flinders Street (1890). The last-named was designed in association with Charles D'Ebro. Further afield the list is a long one, including St Peter's Parsonage, Eastern Hill (1886);

89

Princess Theatre, Spring Street (1886), architect William Pitt, altered in 1922 by A.H. Walkley. Pitt was an active, sportive, political Victorian, and could design to suit the occasion. Here the occasion demanded a French Baroque extravaganza to suit a theatre-loving people

The Winfield Building (left, Speight and D'Ebro, 1893) and Rialto (right, William Pitt, 1890). These buildings and the South Australian Insurance building and the Olderfleet remind us of the eccentricities and imagination of the Victorians. Full of artistic fantasy, they capture many qualities often lacking in modern work

heyday of 'Marvellous Melbourne' and many grandstands were built, such as the South Melbourne Cricket Club grandstand in Albert Park by W.E. Wells (1888).

To sum up, Pitt has been described as a sensitive draftsman (we still have many of his drawings) and a competent 'Gothicist'. In the imaginitive character of some of his buildings we can see something of the inspiration of Ruskin's stones of Venice.

Another category of building of the 1880s was the temperance hotel or coffee palace. It arose from the very vigorous promotion of temperance at that time and the need for accommodation and refreshment for the ordinary non-affluent citizen. (The Temperance and General Society was founded in 1876.) Ellerker, Kilburn and Pitt designed the Federal Coffee Palace (demolished) in Collins Street in 1887. The building had 500 rooms, including 350 bedrooms. There were five Waygood—Otis suspended-type hydraulic elevators and all the latest conveniences of the 1880s. It was crowned by a dome framed in angle-iron. It had 4½ miles (7 kilometres) of bell-wire, 16 miles (26 kilometres) of skirting, 5 miles (8 kilometres) of gas piping and 5 million bricks, to quote a few popular statistics.

The Hotel Windsor, designed by Charles Webb, began as the Grand Coffee Palace in 1886-87, adjacent to the Old White Hart. (The White Hart on the corner of Spring Street and Bourke Streets was replaced at the end of the century by a three-storey brick building which in its turn was demolished in the 1960s to make way for the modern extension of the Windsor). Promoted by a

St Kilda Town Hall (1888); Victoria Brewery, East Melbourne (1896); and the Shire Hall at Werribee (1893). Following the Depression there was much work for sport and racing clubs, including the Melbourne Cricket Ground (1904-13), and grounds at Williamstown (1904-34), Flemington (1913-18) and Caulfield (1914-26). This takes us up to Pitt's death in 1918, when the work was carried on by Albion Walkley. Theatres and racing were important in the

company formed in 1885, coffee palaces were built around the Melbourne area. Queen's Coffee Palace, by Terry and Oakden, was built in 1888 on the corner of Victoria and Rathdowne Streets on a base of Malmsbury bluestone. It has since been demolished, to be replaced by a finance company. The Royal East Melbourne Coffee Palace was designed by Tappin, Gilbert and Dennehy in 1886 and still stands at 74 Hotham Street, East Melbourne. The Royal

Part of the east elevation of the Rialto showing the ironwork and Gothic windows

Hotel Windsor, Spring Street (1886-87). Designed by Charles Webb, this is a very rich building as shown in this close view of the loggia arcading

Park Coffee Palace in Brunswick was designed by Evander McIver in 1888 and the Windsor Coffee Palace by G. McMullen in 1889.

Besides temperance, there abounded many Romantic, Protestant and liberal attitudes, urging all men to become good, wise, prosperous and responsible. One means towards this end was the movement for Mechanics' Institutes. Initiated in Scotland in 1823 by Dr Birkbeck, the Mechanics' Institute was designed to provide education for the 'steam intellect' society, and its success in the industrial areas of Britain was phenomenal. An Institute was built in nearly every town, containing a meeting hall and stage, to promote the idea of education for all, especially popular adult education. Learning, culture and knowledge were the tools for building the ideal society. (The Institutes, however, did not maintain this high ideal and changed to social activities later in the century, becoming useful general-purpose halls.)

The philanthropic societies and movements in nineteenth-century Melbourne created the need for halls where many could meet together and hear a speaker. One of the few remaining is Storey Hall, built for the Hibernian Society and now part of the Royal Melbourne Institute of Technology. Designed by Tappin, Gilbert and Dennehy in 1887, it is little altered and is an example of a hall with galleries on three sides, still retaining its decoration and kauri handrails. It sits solidly on a bluestone basement floor supporting arched fireproof ceilings. As in many a classical front of its day, the main cornice is

91

Queen Bess Row, 74 Hotham Street, East Melbourne (1886), architects Tappin, Gilbert and Dennehy. Built by A.J. Muller of Hawthorn, this building, initially, was the Royal East Melbourne Coffee Palace and has obvious similarities to other coffee palaces. The company failed and the building was converted to three separate apartments

cement render run over a 3-inch (7.5 centimetre) deep slab of cantilevered slate and corbelled moulded brickwork.

This was also the age of the grand hotel, which developed as a natural outcome of the expanding railway network. In most suburbs such a hotel can be found close to the main road and railway station. It was customarily a brick structure of two or three storeys with stables to the rear. Typical of many are Douta Galla Hotel in Newmarket, Brunswick Hotel, the Grandview and Tower Hotels in Alphington, the Aberdeen Hotel in North Fitzroy, the Albion Family Hotel in Northcote, the Palace Hotel in Camberwell, Malone's Hotel in Canterbury and, on the Cobb and Co. route up the Yarra valley, the Grand Hotel at Yarra Glen. All these were built towards the end of the eighties and encapsulated in bricks and mortar something of the sociology and hospitality patterns of late-Victorian Melbourne.

Architects of the day had an appreciation of the fine arts, a sound knowledge of building construction and a relentless desire to stretch the height of the load-bearing wall to its ultimate. This is seen in impressive warehouse construction in the port area and in South Melbourne, as a reflection of the early nineteenth century warehouses in the ports of London and Liverpool. Later in the century fire-resistant floors were often constructed by using 'Terra Cotta Lumber', a mixture of clay and sawdust, made in Brunswick by the Victoria Terra Cotta Company. The material was produced as blocks and arched between iron

92

beams. Many new materials were becoming available in the building industry. Ernest and Alfred Wunderlich set up in Sydney as manufacturers of building materials and by 1890 their factory at Redfern was producing roofing tiles, pressed metal ceilings and asbestos cement sheeting, threatening, inevitably, the traditional plastering trade. In many buildings moulded metal ceilings were replacing lath and plaster, an instance of a factory process replacing an on-site trade

skill.

Industrial structures were simple and functional and there was a high standard of technology for building tall chimneys. Coop's shot tower in Knox Place, completed in 1891, although derelict, is still admired as a fine piece of modelling in brickwork. Further, a device for climbing chimneys, known as a 'creeping frame', was invented in 1887.

The Australia Building (the recently

Bunswick Post Office, an ornate public building on a restricted site, dating from the 1880s

The Shot Tower, Knox Place (1888-91). Built for Walter Coop, who was in business since the early 1850s, this is the only historic shot tower in Victoria. Although a purely 'functional' structure, its play of brick surfaces can be visually appreciated since the demolition of buildings on the site of Museum Station

demolished A.P.A. Building on the corner of Elizabeth Street and Flinders Lane) was designed by Oakden, Addison and Kemp, in association with John Beswicke. (Kemp was a new arrival from Glasgow.) It was a spectacular design for its day (1888-89)—twelve storeys high and 173 feet (53 metres) above the footpath—built when the 'Lane' was the centre of Manchester, textile and floor-covering warehouses. The external walls were solid brick alternating in layers with Stawell stone on a 3-foot (1 metre) thickness of solid Gabo Island granite at the base. The entire area of the site was laid with solid concrete 6 feet (nearly 2 metres) thick, lined with slate and asphalt as a precaution against damp, and the basement was lined with boiler plate. The internal columns were cast iron and the beams built up of boiler plate and angle iron. All except three concrete floors were framed with oregon joists and Baltic flooring. The 220 offices were connected by speaking tube with the entrance hall.[16] 'The hydraulic lifts were propelled to the tenth floor by direct drive pistons which required a 120 feet [37 metres] deep shaft. The shaft was lined with brick and concrete and sunk below the level of the bed of the Yarra.'[17] Described in the press of the day as 'Queen Anne architecture', it was the tallest office building in Australia for sixty years, and obviously predated the city's height restrictions and fire regulations.

The terrace house reached the peak of its popularity before the general demand for a completely detached house in the ever-expanding suburbs which became the

93

APA (Australia) Building, corner Elizabeth Street and Flinders Lane (1888), architects Oakden, Addison and Kemp. This twelve-storey building was the first high-rise structure in Melbourne, and pushed the concept of the load-bearing wall to the limit. By our standards it was hardly fire-resistant, but had much of the technology which made high-rise building feasible

94

Blanche Terrace, 169-179 Victoria Parade, Fitzroy (1867-68). An arcaded terrace of fashionable town houses of the mid-century. The arcading adds rythm to the design

Australian counterpart to the American dream at the turn of the century of a home open to the prairies. Some terraces were designed by architects and some by speculative builders who saw terrace housing as a profitable investment throughout the middle-class suburbs—Carlton, Parkville, Fitzroy, East Melbourne, St Kilda and Albert Park. There was much variety, from Blanch Terrace in Fitzroy (1867-68) with its arcaded treatment to Queen's Mansions in St Kilda

(1889) which were fitted with lifts and electric light. Many of them were left untenanted during the depression of the nineties and later converted into boarding houses which contributed to the social depression of the area.

Parliament Place (Tasma Terrace), by Charles Webb, was built between 1879 and 1886 and is a fine example of a three-storey terrace on sloping ground, a type rare in Melbourne. As the National Trust put it,

'The relationship between the building, street, trees and small park makes this a precinct of great charm'. The most unique would be Clarendon Terrace in East Melbourne, which was commenced in 1857. These three houses are faced by a colonnade rising through two storeys.

As in Regency times the English terrace house had received its final touch in a balcony of wrought iron set against the plain wall face as a delicate foil, so the

95

Tasma Terrace, Parliament Place (1879-86), architect Charles Webb. An unpretentious terrace of houses on a sloping site. This elevation enhances the precinct beside Parliament House, its cast iron lacework expressing the charm of the late-Victorian era. It has been restored and now houses the National Trust

Clarendon Terrace, East Melbourne, commenced in 1857. An unusual example of the giant order adding grace and dignity to a terrace

Australian house of the 1870s and 1880s was enriched by the lacework of decorative cast iron panels so well described and illustrated in Graeme Robertson's books.[18] Cast iron decoration was produced by local foundries soon after the gold rush and was later produced in great quantity for verandah balustrading, valences and spandril brackets. Seen as lacework on a verandah and echoed in shadows on the wall, this was the final touch, as it had been in New Orleans, setting a tone and creating a value. Unpretentious terrace houses can be seen all around the inner suburbs and pre-eminently in South Parkville, a pocket of nineteenth-century housing that represents the variety of types and standards common to the period.

For the perceptive the study of the architecture of those days is a mirror of the life, the aspirations, the value systems, or, as the Germans would say, the *lebensgefuhl* of the period. In spite of the founding and fostering of fortunes in a capitalist economy, there was much philanthropy, and Victorian sentiment was manifest in self-sacrifice, liberal acts and noble gestures. For all its faults the Victorian age was permeated with moral fervour.

In 1869 George Coppin was instrumental in founding the Old Colonists' Homes in North Fitzroy and a year later the first five cottages were built in bluestone, with communal kitchens and bathrooms. Over the years cottages have been added to this estate (Rushall Park) in various styles, some incorporating Dutch gables and polychrome brickwork, and today 'those homes are the

Benvenuta, now Medley Hall, 48 Drummond Street, Carlton. Built in 1892-93 by architect Walter Law, for Lowel Abrahams, small arms manufacturer. Though lacking in 'good taste' as street architecture, this building shows remarkable detailing, such as the double-hung sash windows fabricated on the curve

nearest approach to a real answer to an old age of dignity, comfort and freedom'.[19] Coppin, a man of much enterprise, also proposed a city square between Prince's Bridge and St Paul's Cathedral and opened up Sorrento for tourism.

On a larger scale the Kew Asylum (Willsmere Hospital), built in the grand manner, was opened in 1872 to receive 418 patients divided into three groups: paying, pauper and criminal. The two great towers 80 feet

Willsmere Hospital, Kew (1865-72), designed by Connolly Norman. The front entrance of this great complex of buildings showing the monumental approach to institutional design

Entrance of Benvenuta showing the highly ornate classical treatment

(24 metres) high were designed, but never used, for water storage. The bricks were made on the site, the strings and arches were of Kangaroo Point freestone and the planning is similar to asylums at Ararat and Beechworth.

After the Education Act of 1872 there was a steady supply of public money for building schools and in the next thirty years there was a variety of designs from many architects. The early designs were Gothic, due to the traditional association of church and education, and include the Lee Street State School, Carlton (1873), Faraday Street State School, Carlton (1876) and Wilson Street School, Brighton (1875), the last two by Reed and Barnes. Later, at the turn of the century and after, architects were freer in the use of secular styles, incorporating Queen Anne features, larger windows, more attractive brickwork and terra cotta. Such a building is the Surrey Hills State School in Beatrice Avenue, designed by H.R. Bastow in 1890. Generally school planning reflected the education policies of the day—a regimented classroom system, corridors and broad entrances so that children could be marched in.

From the point of view of interior architecture the three finest interiors are the Legislative Council Chamber (begun 1856), the Law Courts Library (begun 1875) and the Head Office of the Commercial Bank of Australia, 335 Collins Street. The first two have already been referred to. The bank building was built in 1891 by Lloyd Tayler and Alfred Dunn, architects in association. The frontage of this building was recon-

Faraday Street State School, Carlton (1876), designed by Reed and Barnes, provided for 800 pupils in its two storeys of austere brickwork, relieved by a square central tower and turret roofs at each end

structed in 1941 but the banking chamber was left intact. It is a great octagonal space on the Renaissance principle of geometric harmony of proportions, and is roofed with intersecting ribs in brickwork, creating a dome 60 feet (18 metres) in diameter. Above is a great lantern with a system of mirrors which gives the impression of expanding space. As an essay in the handling of light and space it is one of the greatest interiors of the Victorian era in existence. Professor Joseph Burke described it as:

> one of the rare examples of the Pantheon idea—a great centralising enclosure of space—in Melbourne. Kenneth Clark has described this idea as the Romans' greatest contribution to western architecture. In its ornamental scale it complements the grandeur of the Reading Room in the Public Library. Victorian architecture is coming into its own, and if we destroy this, posterity will never forgive us.[20]

The building is now safe from demolition.

Of greater significance in the field of building technology were the great warehouses, engine sheds, brick kilns and other industrial structures. An expanding capitalist economy demanded them, but their chief interest lay in their bridging the years between time-honoured construction methods and the new iron and steel technology. Their perimeter walls were load-bearing but cast iron stanchions and either wrought iron or oregon timber were used in spanning members.

Within the city the most impressive of these structures was the great warehouse built for the New Zealand Loan and Mercantile Agency between Collins Street and Flinders Lane, near Spencer Street, (sometimes known as the Asmic Warehouse). It was designed by Lloyd Tayler in 1883 and sadly is now demolished. Its powerful arcading in brickwork rising through five floors reminded us of the great railway viaducts recently completed at that time. Many warehouses were built on a smaller scale in Flinders Lane, situated as it was between the port and the retail centre of Melbourne, but few have such an uncompromising approach towards honesty of design as the Asmic Warehouse. With the emphasis on the design of the facade it was thought that a neo-classical frontage was correct. Anyway, it was acceptable to the client, and for many architects these buildings kept the bread on the table.

Opposite the Asmic Warehouse in Collins

Williamstown Grammar School, 66-67 The Strand, Williamstown (1887). This house on a wide bluestone base structure is unusual for its brickwork, chimneys and cast iron lacework, all with a slightly Gothic touch

Street is the Edwards Dunlop Building, built by Charles Webb in 1872. This was originally the Sands and McDougall warehouse. Built solidly on a bluestone base, it has had successive storeys added to it by Oakden and Ballantyne and Hare and Hare.

Charles Webb designed Flinders House (238-44 Flinders Lane) in 1870 in brickwork with a rendered facade on the street; Frank Stapley designed the Bible Society building (241-3) in 1898 in brickwork on a Malmsbury bluestone base; Sulman and Power designed Royston House (247-51) at the same date, with a highly original Art Nouveau mannerist elevation, and M.W. and F.B. Tompkins designed Lane Centre (325-31) in 1907 in brickwork with exposed oregon sawtooth roof trusses.

Then there are the bluestone warehouses, commencing with Seabrook House, 573-7 Lonsdale Street (1858). Goldsbrough Mort Wool Store (1861) on the corner of Bourke and William Streets was mentioned in Chapter 3. Sigma Warehouse, 562-76 Flinders Lane, was built in 1874, having four storeys and an axed bluestone facade.

In Lonsdale Street George Jobbins built the Victoria Bond (565-71) in 1887 in brickwork with an internal iron frame, and Twentyman and Askew, in association with F.G. Green, built the Lonsdale Free Store (541-51) in 1890, a brick warehouse of six storeys.

The most picturesque, because you can only side-glance them in a narrow lane, are the warehouses in Niagara Lane, built by G.de Lacy Evans in 1887. Each goods entrance (one above the other) was provided with an American barrel-hoist, protected from above with little penthouses. Built with Northcote facing bricks and Preston whites with accents of Oamaru stone, this elevation has great charm. The basement is laid with Forbes' Patent Compo pavement and all the other floors are Tasmanian ironbark.[21]

Of all the industrial structures, perhaps the great brick kilns are the most interesting. The Hoffman Brick and Pottery Company commenced operating in 1870 and the first Hoffman kiln, which was circular and located in Brunswick, came into operation in 1872. The Northcote Brick Company, one of the largest brickworks in the Melbourne area, built five Hoffman kilns on their site during the 1880s and the discovery of a reef of fine white clay enabled them to make fancy bricks and pipes. Business prospered till the mid-1890s, when orders plummeted so drastically that the company only survived by combining with others.

These kilns, now demolished, were beautiful structures with brick-built vaulted tunnels continuing round either side and the two semi-circular ends of each kiln. An opportunity for imaginative recycling was lost, but, at the time of writing, the clay mill, a magnificent brick structure with oregon sawtooth roofing, still survives.

A number of Hoffman kilns still survive—those of the Clifton Brick Company in Dawson Street, Brunswick, and Railway Parade West, Preston; City Brickworks in Tooronga Road and Elizabeth Street, Malvern; Oakleigh Brickworks in Stamford Road, Oakleigh; and Glen Iris Bricks in Templestowe Road, Bulleen, which has the largest and most recently constructed kiln (1955-56).

Down by the waterfront two magnificent cargo sheds between Spencer Street Bridge and the *Polly Woodside*, known as wharf buildings one and two, were built in 1891.

Some of the features which make Melbourne a special and sensitive city are (or were) the street-front shop windows of Collins Street and the intimate shopping arcades, beautiful enclosures with a gracious sense of human scale that run approximately north-south through the city centre. Such are Royal Arcade, 331-339 Bourke Street, by Charles Webb (1869 and added to during the period 1901-23 by Hyndman and Bates), and Block Arcade, 280-286 Collins Street, by Twentyman and Askew (1890-93).

There is much more to describe. A walk around the city reveals the rich variety of High Victorian facades, like G.de Lacy Evans's highly Baroque Sum Kum Lee building, 112-114 Little Bourke Street (1887-88), and Thomas Watts's Robb's Building (1885) on the corner of Collins and King Streets opposite the Federal Coffee Palace. John Robb, who owned Coonac in Toorak, went bankrupt and the bank was forced to foreclose on the half-finished building. This was the heady stuff of Victorian Melbourne.

No account of late-Victorian Melbourne would be complete without reference to its railways, for it was the railway stations reflecting a railway age that held up a mir-

ror of late nineteenth-century building techniques. On the multi-storey timber signal boxes, the great masonry engine sheds, but above all on the stations were lavished all that presented a good 'face' to the public and promoted respectable rail travel. Indeed, they had the image that airport terminals have today, and there were good reasons for this.

For the Victorians, and for reasons going back deep into the Industrial Revolution, the railways had come to be regarded as symbolic of the inevitable progress of a Christian civilization, a sort of prestige thing; in the days of absolute moral values the station-master had a very respectable position, and this explains, for instance, the scandal and the revulsion caused by the Great Train Robbery in England in the last century. Whereas the railway stations of England are eclectic in style, those in Melbourne are more often than not standard patterns for which private architects were not employed, but they reflected good building construction using richly a wide variety of the building materials available.

Take South Melbourne (1887), for instance, with its cantilevered roof awning frame finishing up under the platform with a 'toe' constructed of railway lines and red gum sleepers. Here is a marvellous station with floors of kauri on red deal bearers, walls enriched with red bricks, white bricks, dark Hawthorns and dressings of Waurn Ponds stone. It has a timber panelled roof over the public lobby and ornamental work externally of cast iron and zinc.

Again, Clifton Hill (1888) is stately in its

Sum Kum Lee building, 112 Little Bourke Street (1887-88), a Baroque fantasy designed by G. de Lacy Evans

ceiling heights and well provided with open fires, no longer lit for the comfort of travellers. It has Oamaru stone dressings, red deal flooring and a wonderful system of leading cast iron rainwater down-pipes through the cast iron platform columns and into the stormwater drains.

Lastly, Spencer Street Administration Building (1890) is a colossus designed by James Moore and built as a result of the Gillies-Deakin government's unrealistic and

Goods office building, Spencer Street (1880s). A good example of rubbed brick arch work and details, but there is some Victorian coarseness of design in the porch feature

extravagant Railways Bill. This surely sums it all up. The huge brick, stucco-covered building, now in a bad state of repair, has monumental halls and corridors and a main bifurcated staircase of bluestone steps, cast iron balusters and hardwood handrail finely moulded which is nothing short of palatial. In the inevitable march of Victorian civilization it is little wonder that every Victorian schoolboy wanted to be an engine-driver.

High Victorian Melbourne was a vigorous, progressive city. There is a recognized tendency for each age to idealize the preceding one. As the Victorians looked back on Georgian England with nostalgia so do we with Australian Victoriana, and we are indulgent of its faults. In his *Town Life in Australia*, Richard Twopeny was one of those writers responsible for the legend of Australia as a cultural desert. Indeed, as Geoffrey Serle comments, 'intellect and the arts, until very recent times, at least, have been almost the last things a European has associated with Australia'.[22]

However, in the 1880s this was far from being the case. The designers of the last century might often have lacked a sense of humour, but the buildings they created, sometimes hideous, sometimes romantic, are rich in the flavour of their age. As Lewis Mumford said of their American contemporaries, Charles McKim and Daniel Burnham, 'the age shaped them and chose them and used them for its ends. Their mode of building was almost inescapably determined by the milieu in which they worked'.[23]

Australian Club, 110 William Street (1879-80). A building redolent with the opulence and rich culture of the age, expressing Melbourne as the intellectual centre of Australia

103

Between 1891 and 1895 Melbourne experienced a slump matched only by the Depression of 1930. Banks crashed, production fell by about 30 per cent and thousands were unemployed and financially ruined. The prosperity of the previous decade vanished in falling prices and the bankruptcy of land and loan companies. A sharp fall in rents and demand for real estate spelt an end to the speculator and affected the building industry. The Victorian census of 1891 recorded 16 000 vacant dwellings and by 1894 over 20 000 were vacant in Melbourne alone.

The period of 'Marvellous Melbourne' was over and by 1895 the population had fallen to 430 000 from a peak of more than half a million. There was keen competitive tendering for each job and builders lived from hand to mouth. Cockram's were successful in tendering for the Eastern Hill Fire Station (1892). This was the design of Lloyd Tayler and Fitts, in conjunction with Smith and Johnson, and its dominating feature was an early Italian campanile with a tray-like balcony. 'By a most ingenious system of electrical mechanism the opening of the doors gives the signal to the firemen, drops the collars on the horses' heads and raises the gates in the stables.'[1]

In the city, Goode House, 395 Collins Street, was designed by Wright, Reed and Beaver (1892), and in 1893 the Equitable Building on the corner of Collins and Elizabeth Streets (now replaced by the C.M.L. Building) was begun. This was designed by Edward Raht of New York and built with American money. It was a power-

Chapter 6

Federation Architecture

To forget the past would be as foolish as to ignore the future. Behind is custom, as in front is adventure.
W.R. Lethaby

ful and impressive monument using red granite from Phillip Island. Its huge entrance arch rose through four floors and framed a group of bronze statuary 13 feet (4 metres) high and cast in Vienna.[2] One or two private mansions like The Towers, Pakington Street, Kew (1890), St Leonards, Milan Street, Mentone (1892), and Stonnington, Glenferrie Road, Malvern (1892), were built; but with loan money from London desiccated, large public works pro-

grammes stagnated.

Although the foregoing buildings were in many ways the Victorian mixture as before, new movements from Europe were affecting Australia, merging into a way of design which made the buildings of the turn of the century quite different from those of the 1880s. In 1893 the City Architect of Sydney submitted four sets of designs for the new George Street Markets—Gothic, Queen Anne, American Romanesque and Italian Renaissance. New movements, trends and fashions encouraged eclecticism and a degree of excitement among designers. The influences that brought this about can be briefly summarized as follows.

First there was the influence of William Morris and the Arts and Crafts Movement which affected design, buildings, furniture and wallpaper. Secondly, Rossetti and Burne-Jones and the Pre-Raphaelite Movement influenced all art, including stained glass and the use of colour, and injected a strain of moral seriousness into it. Thirdly, the far-reaching effect of Art Nouveau gathered strength in Europe after 1890. This was a very significant, sensitive and short-lived fashion in decoration affecting the work of architects—Louis Sullivan in Chicago, Victa Horta and Henri Van de Velde in Brussels, Antoni Gaudi in Barcelona, Annesley Voysey in England and Charles Mackintosh in Scotland.

Architecturally these influences were reflected in the style known as Queen Anne which was initiated in England by Norman Shaw, featuring red brickwork and white-painted woodwork. Shaw was in partner-

ship with Eden Nesfield and produced some highly picturesque country mansions like Leys Wood (1868) in Sussex which were sensitively related to the landscape in a total design. Their mature style, or more correctly Shaw's, was to be seen in some London town houses which used the style of William and Mary and Queen Anne as a period source. This is what became an international success. This decorative 'fun' architecture became popular in America, but,

Eastern Hill Fire Station, East Melbourne (1893), designed by Lloyd Tayler and Fitts. This was an up-to-date fire station, yet with some Mannerist, or Queen Anne, touches. The tower is a controlling feature in the composition

(Detail) A close-up of the tower with its playful balcony and lantern

as David Saunders comments, 'The house which Australians call a Queen Anne house is not to be found elsewhere. It is related to both English and American architecture, but distinct from both'.[3]

The popularity of the Queen Anne style in Australia coincided with Federation (some called it the Federation Style). The rising feeling of nationalism was manifesting itself in architecture as a quest for a uniquely Australian style respecting climate and local conditions. The *fin de siècle* was characterized by a tremendous enthusiasm for Australian uniqueness.

[The name Queen Anne] tends to rub off on all that happened in the period. It is a name that had international currency but meant different things in different places. The style it refers to in this country is uniquely Australian. In the leading examples it represented a fundamentally new architecture.[4]

The style was a significant step in the movement, involving a total integration of the building with its site. Buildings were seen in three dimensions with a due regard for landscaping.

The brick manufacturers who had survived the depression were now meeting the demand for red bricks rather than multicolours. It was usual at the turn of the century to lay them with mortar to match the brick colour struck flush and then clearly articulate the joint with a thin line of white mortar recessed in. This was known as tuck pointing. A shipment of Marseilles tiles had arrived from France in 1886 and heralded a change in roofing patterns which has lasted till today.

Queen Anne houses were characterized by irregularity of plan and massing; broken gables and roof shapes terminating in terra cotta ridge tiles and fantastic dragons; polygonal bay windows and turned timber verandah posts, usually painted white. Octagonal 'towers' or corner bay windows were finished with candle-snuffer roofs. Curved timber bressumers arched between turned posts and there were picket fences along the street frontage, also painted white.

In Sydney there was a closer link with American architecture. The new movement in home design was called the balcony style and sometimes a sleepout was incorporated in the gable end of a generously pitched tile roof. In Melbourne the houses were more closely related to the landscape. Several architects, strongly influenced by this new feeling, became well-known.

Henry Kemp and Beverley Ussher were both born in England. (Until this time most Australian architects were English-born and English-trained. It is only in this century that we are beginning to feel the strength of Australian-born architects, locally trained through the system of articles.) Kemp had an interest in medieval buildings and a love of sketching. His first partnership was with Oakden and Addison. Ussher worked first with Walter Butler, who designed Billila in Halifax Street, Brighton, in 1905 and later joined Kemp in a partnership which was prolific in the production of Queen Anne houses for a clientele of professional or upper middle-class people.

In Kew, 7 Adeney Avenue (1907) is a typical product of this partnership. The house has curved timber bressumers between coupled turned posts and beautiful modulations of light and dark in each room. The projections in plan shape give the house subdued light punctuated with brighter areas. Kemp built 5 Adeney Avenue in 1912 for himself and it is beautifully integrated with the landscape.

Ellerker and Kilburn's design for Tara in Studley Park Road, built in 1887, was a magnificent example of Queen Anne architecture—fantastic and imaginitive—but tragically it has disappeared. It seemed to have an affinity with American Queen Anne and could be compared with, say, the house where Mark Twain lived in Connecticut. At 28 Studley Park Road (1912) is a house by Christopher Cowper, perhaps less sensitive than the work of Kemp and Ussher, but crowned with a magnificent terra cotta dragon.

This new type of house went up all around the suburbs at the turn of the century and continued on till the First World War. Among the architects producing designs for Queen Anne houses were Thomas Inskip, Christopher Cowper, I.G. Beaver, H.W. and F.B. Tompkins, Oakden and Ballantyne, Klingender and Alsop, A.H. Fisher, A.W. Purnell, William Blackett, A.E.H. Carleton and George de Lacy Evans. The last-named also designed a memorial for those fallen in the Boer War. This is a little structure in brown Pyrmont sandstone in St Kilda Road, modelled in Perpendicular Gothic.

106

107

7 Adeney Avenue, Kew (1910), architects Kemp and Ussher. A fine example of the Queen Anne style in Melbourne featuring red brickwork, decorative timber cladding, turned posts and curved timber bressumers arching between them

Two big houses call for special comment: Tay Creggan in Yarra Street, Hawthorn (1897) by Guyon Purchas, and Campion College, Studley Park Road (1906), probably by Kemp. Tay Creggan is a fantasy more Elizabethan than anything else and contains, amongst other rich features, a room roofed with arched trusses, each one seated on a carved dragon corbel in timber. Between each truss is a stained glass dome. Campion College, more regular in plan, shows a fine sense of materials: sandstone, brick, tile-hanging, parquetry and stained glass. According to David Saunders,

These pictures are of Tara, Studley Park Road, Kew (1888, demolished 1959), architects Ellerker and Kilburn. Built at the height of the boom, this house differs strikingly from its Italianate contemporaries. This is a large house of red brick and terra cotta and an early example of the Queen Anne style, revealing the influence of houses in San Francesco, Chicago and New York at that time. The tiles are of Roman pattern, not Marseilles

If 1886 can be taken as the beginning of the new style, leaving aside whether properly called Queen Anne or Proto-Queen Anne, in view of significant contemporaries, the end of it was already in sight by 1900.[5]

This was the year that Robert Haddon arrived in Melbourne, fully immersed in Art Nouveau as a way of design, to find work with Purchas and Teague. Two years later he was in practice on his own. As chief lecturer in architecture at the Working Men's College (now R.M.I.T.), he taught, wrote and sketched much. His strength was his appreciation of materials and their honest application (the 'preciousness of materials', as John Ruskin put it). Anything 'stuck on' or applied was wrong. He appreciated Australian sunlight, flora and fauna and the local brickwork. 'In all the products of the clay kiln we do well, and have done well.

Our bricks and our terra cottas are most lasting and reliable, and long may we continue to use such materials and see to their increase'.[6]

Haddon brought a freshness and strength to the Melbourne architectural scene. In a paper read to the Victorian Institute of Architects he made such pleas as,

Seek truth. Be true to your materials. Study mass. Let nature do all she can

110

Campion College, 99 Studley Park Road, Kew (1906), architect probably Henry Kemp. This is a magnificent Queen Anne house showing sensitive detailing and a fine feeling for materials—brick, sandstone, terra cotta work, timbers and stained glass

Anselm, 4 Glenferrie Street, Caulfield (1906). Built by Robert Haddon for himself. With few exceptions, everything about this house is original, including the built-in fittings and the hardware, so it is a good record of the architect's design philosophy. This view shows the wrought iron over the gateway and the octagonal turret

with the exteriors, with her sunlight and her shadows. Study colour and its harmonies. Know the unfailing value of a plain surface. If you ornament, know the value of clustered enrichments.
Never be afraid of simplicity.

Haddon had little conscience about the suburban sprawl. 'The housement of, say, Carlton or Malvern, or West Melbourne and Balwyn, by contrast, will show that we have passed from the old country idea of the terraced house, built right on to the street frontage, to the open air type of the garden city.'[7] Balwyn was largely paddock land then and was ready for the 'garden city' concept.

In his many houses in the expanding suburbs (for instance his own house, 4 Glenferrie Street, Caulfield, 1906) he exemplified principles new for those days. He recommended the free plan and elimination of the drawing room. 'The "meal-room" may be made a subsection of the livingroom by means of a semi-open screen, or by making of it a bay or ingle.' In his own house we can see a large living area with his study opening off it. On the corner of the living area is an octagonal bay and on the street frontage the garage, the last instance where this was permitted in Caulfield. The car age had hardly arrived.

Imported fashions were absorbed by a vigorous building industry and adapted to suit a new environment. Something of the freshness of Art Nouveau was lost in the naturalization process. As Robin Boyd said: 'The flow and sensitivity had not survived the ocean trip'.[8] The fashion helped the terra cotta industry; firms like W.H. Rocke and Co. produced new designs. Among architects there was a movement towards an indigenous Australian 'style' rather than the repeated echo of European trends. Building design was still largely derivative and the most that can be admitted was a measure of adaptation, or an 'Australianization'. At 54 Bowen Crescent, Princes Hill (1900), and at 93 Elizabeth Street, Richmond (c.1882), for instance, the terra cotta dragon on the ridge has changed to a terra cotta kangaroo and, crowning the parapet of the strange Gothic facade of 313-15 Drummond Street, Carlton, built by Oakden, Addison and Kemp in 1889, are four chimeras with kangaroo-like bodies. Terra cotta decoration often featured Australian flora and fauna, as seen on the front of the Old Municipal Library on the corner of Toorak Road and Osborne Street in South Yarra (1893), a picturesque combination of Scottish Baronial and American Romanesque, designed by John Thomas Keleeher of the Department of Works. In one church only, St Andrew's Prestyterian, Skipton, were kangaroos used as gargoyles.

Eastbourne House (1901) was supposedly another Haddon building, although tenders were called for it by Sydney Smith and Ogg. It is an asymmetrical composition incorporating his favourite features: the corner tower or turret, the plain surfaces and their pilaster strips, the repetitive terra cotta ornament, the sinuous carving in the gable, a fantasy of wrought iron work in the balustrades and the lion's head over the entrance. Lions' heads were also featured at 243 Collins Street (1920s), a symmetrical city elevation. This was a face-lift, but it clearly showed Haddon's hand as a designer. The iron balustrading to the stairs is carefully designed and dark green faience tiles face the frontage and line the lift and stair well.

Haddon designed three notable churches. In chronological order they are Malvern Presbyterian, Wattletree Road (1906); St Stephen's Presbyterian, Balaclava Road, Caulfield (1910); and St Andrew's, on the corner of Palmer and Drummond Streets, Oakleigh (1928). In the first two there is fine brickwork in the buttressing and openings and simple trusses under a roof lined with Californian red pine. The Malvern church is roofed with Vermont green slates and both have 'Decorated' tracery of a sort, with some Art Nouveau feeling. The Oakleigh church is asymmetrical, having a corner feature of an octagonal turret and fleche.

Milton House, 25 Flinders Lane (1900-02), was designed as a private hospital for Dr William Moore by Sydney Smith and Ogg. Its chief interest lies not so much in its design as a hospital (though it is an example of an Edwardian hospital) but in its Art Nouveau decoration. The sinuous curves of the ironwork in the fanlight and balconies over the main entrance are distinctly French and all the details of this building (the repetitive terra cotta work, the generous eaves overhang and the chimneys linked over the ridge of the roof with a brick arch) are entirely in keeping with its style and period.

Nocklofty, 551 Royal Parade (1891). This house, recently threatened with demolition, has wonderfully rich timber carving inside and out

Above: 45-47 Spring Street, a fine example of Art Nouveau design right in the city, with terra cotta ornament and wrought iron work. It was built at the turn of the century, but has been demolished (Architects Purchas and Teague)

Front gable of Nocklofty, showing clearly the carving and detailing. Note, too, the semi-circular brick arches, suggesting the influence of American Romanesque

115

Left: 313 and 315 Drummond Street, Carlton (1889).
This town house which used to have a verandah was
designed by Oakden, Addison and Kemp for W.G.
Welsh of Ball and Welsh. The chimera-like creatures
have dogs' faces, kangaroos' bodies, eagles' claws and
lions' tails

Above: 468, 470 Church Street, Richmond (1908). Art
Nouveau detail in plaster on a bow window

116

*Art Nouveau detail from the Tomasetti Building in
Flinders Lane (elevation C. 1900)*

117

An Art Nouveau decorative motif in plaster from
Tavistock House in Flinders Lane

118

One time South Yarra Post Office, then Municipal
Library, Osborne Street (1893). Some have labelled
this American Romanesque, as reflecting the work of
Louis Sullivan. It also could be described as Scottish
baronial. It has a romantic feeling

*Near left and above: The stucco panels filled with
Australian flora and fauna in relief are evidence of
the concern for an indigenous architecture round
about the time of Federation*

120

Eastbourne House, Wellington Parade, East Melbourne (1920). Supposedly by Robert Haddon, but he could have been responsible for the elevations only. The elevations show a number of influences, including Art Nouveau, and are characterized by a delicate asymmetry. There is fine brickwork, repetitive terra cotta ornament, wrought iron gutter brackets, and, shown in the details, the 'peacock' balcony. As Haddon remarks, 'Each material has its own nature. The best qualities of each may be brought out by true craft labours'

122

St Stephen's Presbyterian Church, Caulfield (1910), architect Robert Haddon. This view emphasizes his original approach to Gothic windows and the admixture of brick and stone dressings

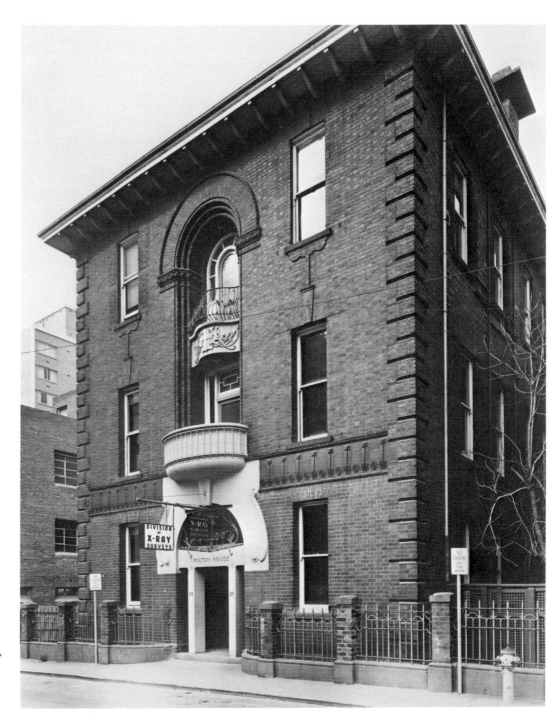

Milton House, 25 Flinders Lane (1900-02). Designed as a private hospital by Smith and Ogg, this is the best example of Art Nouveau work in the city. Particularly noteworthy are the curvaceous ironwork, the repetitive terra cotta decoration, the fine brickwork and the beautifully detailed cornice

123

Another architect and creative designer was a native of Australia, Harold Desbrowe Annear. Extrovert in personality and Bohemian in taste, Annear signed articles with William Salway and became a fashionable and highly successful architect and popular after-dinner speaker. His clients were distinguished and wealthy. His circle of friends included Dame Nellie Melba; Sir Baldwin Spencer, Chief Protector of Aborigines for the Commonwealth; Hardy Wilson, the architect, watercolourist and writer; and the Heidelberg painters W.B. McGuiness and Frederick McCubbin; but not, apparently, his head draftsman who successfully sued him for back pay and one per cent commission on a job.[9] Socially he was popular and during the First World War he involved himself in many and varied fund-raising schemes. He taught surveying at the university and he edited *For Every Man his Home*. His articles in this publication set forth his creative approach to domestic design—his details for fireplaces and windows were unique. He was a good draftsman and some of his sketches appear in the *Australasian Builder and Contractors' News*.

One of his early jobs was an exercise in Greek Doric, the Springthorpe Memorial in Boroondara Cemetery, Kew (1897). This structure reveals a solid classical training and the ability to use correctly a number of different materials: Labrador granite, Carrara marble, bronze and stained glass, merging them into the most remarkable monument in the cemetery. At this time there was a revival of residential stained

124

glass, which had reached its peak in America about 1890. It came about as a result of the Pre-Raphaelite and Gothic Revival handcraft movements merging with late nineteenth-century technology, and some of the finest examples of stained glass can be found in the homes, churches and monuments of this period.

Annear did his most innovative work on three houses built one above the other up the Eyrie, Eaglemont. The first one, at the

The Springthorpe Memorial, Boroondara Cemetery, Kew (1897), architect H. Desbrowe Annear. This is a finely detailed monument incorporating six different marbles, bronze work, stained glass, and sculpture by Bertram McKennel. The Argus described it as 'the most beautiful work of its kind in Australia'

Bendigo Hotel, 125 Johnston Street, Collingwood. Constructed in Edwardian times, this building has many playful Art Nouveau mannerisms (Architects Sydney Smith, Ogg and Serpell)

125

Berkley Hall, 11 Princes Street, St Kilda. Original structure 1853-54, balconies added in the 1920s with decorative details typical of that period

34 The Eyrie, Eaglemont (1903). Desbrowe Annear designed this house with similar feeling to his own house, 38 The Panorama, incorporating an open-plan living area and built-in fittings, which in those days were a new idea

top of the hill (38 The Panorama), was built for him and his bride in 1902 and demonstrates, with its free-flowing plan, his ability to design unrestricted by tradition. Here he entertained lavishly. The other two homes, 34 The Eyrie (1903) and 55 Outlook Drive (1903), are similar in character. For these three houses the site was ideal and Annear made the most of it. They represent his best contribution to home design. Outwardly they show a pleasant informality, half-timbered gables and decorated verandahs, but from the point of view of planning, detailing, built-in fittings and window design Annear hardly excelled them.

He had plenty of opportunity to do so, but his many later houses were designed for a wealthy clientele willing to pay for a classical elegance. They were gracious homes for a leisured suburban class. Two homes in this Heidelberg area have the same informality as those on The Eyrie: 25 Riverside Road (1910) and 234 Rosanna Road (1910), the latter having a beautiful sequence of rooms, built-in fittings, an 'en suite' bathroom and stained glass in the windows; but those in the Toorak area are of a different type, having more stucco and Baroque detailing, fine brickwork, gracious porches and entrance halls and carefully designed chimneys and eaves. Such were 241 (1915) and 249 (1919) Domain Road, South Yarra; 404 Glenferrie Road, Malvern (1920); and, also in the 1920s, 203 Orrong Road, Toorak; Cloyne, 609 Toorak Road; and other houses in Heyington Place.[10]

127

203 Orrong Road, Toorak (1927), view of front entrance. In this house the architect, Desbrowe Annear, displays detailing at its finest, not only in the generous Queen Anne entrance hood, but also in the brickwork, windows and eaves overhang. This was his last house

278 Cotham Road, Kew (demolished). A house by Robert Haddon already in this picture showing signs of wear. The buttresses, wide eaves overhangs and the huge terra cotta dragon give the place a touch of fantasy

Concrete technology was in its infancy, growing rapidly, and its Australian exponents were not lacking. In 1907 John Garnsworthy, an engineer, built The White House on The Strand, Williamstown, of concrete and railway girders, after picking up the idea from American technical literature in the local Mechanics Institute.[11] In 1912 John Monash, in association with George Higgins, built 4 Bay Street, Beaumaris, completely in reinforced concrete, including the pitched roof with its 'purlins' and 'rafters'. In 1913 H.R. Crawford designed a house in Hawthorn with reinforced concrete walls.[12] In those days treatises on the new technology of reinforced concrete were usually written in French or German, so Monash, fluent in these languages, was ahead in this field. His Morrell Bridge, built in reinforced concrete in 1899, was a masterpiece in economy and grace and, though hardly designed for the traffic age, still takes the Anderson Street traffic today. In the early years of this century he and men like Sir Clive Steele raised the standard of civil engineering in this country.

New inventions and labour-saving devices were coming on to the market. The gas fire, the gas bath heater and small gas sink heater were generally accepted; and electricity, the 'clean' fuel (except at Yallourn), was compensating for the shortage of domestic labour. As early as 1904 the first 'all electric' house without chimneys was built at Geelong. Hardie's fibro-cement was introduced as cheap wall cladding and Malthoid was available for near-flat roofing

on the fashionable American-type, or Californian, bungalows.

America was leading the world in the use of structural steel. The Monadnock Building in Chicago (1890-91) was the last of the great masonry towers, but there was a complete absence of classical decoration. Concurrently Louis Sullivan was building the Wainwright in St Louis, using a steel skeleton, while in Melbourne Wright, Reed and Beaver were building Goode House, 395 Collins Street, using external load-carrying walls and a Gothic facade. Similarly the Equitable Building (1893) on the corner of Collins and Elizabeth Streets had load-bearing walls.

Morrell Bridge, Anderson Street, South Yarra (1899), an early reinforced concrete bridge designed by John Monash

It was not only structural framing that made the skyscraper possible. It was the elevator, the telephone, central heating, mechanical ventilation, the revolving door, plumbing, communications systems and an impressive list of mechanical improvements. Melbourne's first tall buildings were serviced by hydraulic elevators, either 'direct action' type or 'suspended', fed by high pressure mains from the Melbourne Hydraulic Power Company. At peak hour most buildings had their own steam or gas-driven pump. Three hundred of these elevators were connected, but inevitably the electric traction elevator took over and by 1903 Otis were making ten electric elevators for every one hydraulic. The lift well was enclosed by an iron lattice and the main stair wound around this within a square well.

Concrete framing was in its developmental stage during the Edwardian era and by the First World War concrete-framed multistorey buildings were accepted. The first reinforced concrete (or 'armoured concrete' as it was then called) buildings to be permitted by the City Council were 2 and 3 Oliver's Lane, built in stages from 1910 onwards, each stage a prosaic exercise in the new technology. In 1913 Love and Lewis's store was built in Chapel Street, Prahran, of reinforced concrete framing and this led to wider acceptance after the War.

Domes were still popular features. The dome of Flinders Street Station has become a Melbourne landmark or meeting place. The design for the station was the subject of a competion in 1899 and the winners were Fawcett and Ashworth. Brick and Harcourt granite were used in this fine Queen Anne-type elevation, which features a dome resembling the Church of the Sorbonne in Paris and a tower terminating the vista down Elizabeth Street. But traditionally architects design buildings and the spaces between them, and the situation of this building and the railway line is nothing short of tragic for the people of Melbourne, who are thus barred from the use and enjoyment of the Yarra River at the very spot where the 'village' started, as they are further up the river by the South-Eastern Freeway.

The dome over the new Reading Room of the State Library was more technologically significant. Designed by Bates, Peebles and Smart, the details of this dome were first prepared in England in 1910, with the reinforced concrete design supplied by John Monash. One hundred and fifteen feet (35 metres) in diameter and constructed with the Kahn System, it was the largest concrete dome in the southern hemisphere at that time (1913). Originally it had 4000 square feet (371 square metres) of glazing, but was found not to be waterproof. Eventually all natural light was excluded by lining the dome with fibrous plaster and sheathing it externally with copper sheet.

A dome which sadly was never built was designed for St George's Church, Rathdowne Street, Carlton, by Reed, Smart and Tappin in 1897.[13] Of all the churches in Melbourne this one, with its grand barrel vault over a rich floor of encaustic tiles, is closest to the atmosphere of the Italian Renaissance church. A prominent dome was that built over the synagogue in St Kilda Road, designed in 1930 by Nahum Barnet. Domes have been built over Greek Orthodox churches since the Second World War and over the Russian Church on the corner of Canning and Dryburgh Streets, North Melbourne, in the 1960s. Nahum Barnet also designed the Auditorium (now the Mayfair) Theatre 167-73 Collins Street in 1913. This theatre, which was added to in the early 1930s by C.N. Hollinshed, has a strongly Queen Anne facade. In the same year (1913) another arcade was added to Melbourne's shopping centre—Centreway, 259-63 Collins Street—by Harry Tompkins.

Since 1855 Melbourne University had grown with a steady accretion of unrelated but individually interesting buildings. Melbourne Teachers' College (State College of Victoria of Melbourne) was built in Grattan Street by the Public Works Department (architect G.H.B. Austin, the designer of Mount Buffalo Chalet). Built in stages from 1888 onwards, the building is unusual for its 'Jacobean Revival' dress in an atmosphere of Victorian romanticism (possibly a reflection of the Royal Holloway College at London University?). The Conservatorium of Music, on Royal Parade, was built by Bates, Peebles and Smart in 1910. Here is another instance of the influence of Art Nouveau. We know more about acoustics today, but its finely designed eaves overhang, perhaps reminiscent of Annesley Voysey's work in England, and sensitive decoration and detailing make it a charming example of its period.

In 1910 Edwardian Melbourne had some

ugly blemishes and there was concern about slums which had been caused by the depression. Socio-economic factors had left their mark on the built environment and these sores had been left to fester. It was reported that in one case there was only 6 feet (less than 2 metres) between the front of a fireplace and the staircase, and in another case two 'Chinamen' had broken a hole through a bedroom wall in desperation to admit more air.[14]

In architectural design the Edwardian period could not be described as elegant. In many ways the sanity of Georgian architecture or even of the colonial period had been lost in a medly of imported mannerisms. Although Edwardian work is appreciated today because the interiors are better lit than those of the previous twenty-five years and made visually interesting by means of fretwork shapes and carving in woodwork and stained glass windows, much of late Victorian and Edwardian architecture was in a chasm of bad taste. It was unaffected by the Modern Movement, which was only embryonic and had not yet made an impact. Some buildings, as we have seen, were charmingly Art Nouveau but many, like fire stations and Salvation Army citadels, were ugly and awkward in scale. There was red brick and brown and cream paint amid classical details distorted by mannerisms and crowned by Dutch gables and restless skylines.

However, at the turn of the century Melbourne acquired some impressive public buildings, namely post offices and court houses, and these are to be found in plenty

131

Melbourne Teachers' College (State College of Victoria at Melbourne), Grattan Street (commenced 1888). Designed by G.H.B. Austin, this building shows the exotic character of the times in a proliferation of features and restless skyline

Palmer's Pavilion, St Kilda Pier. An interesting example of late Victorian timber construction, still being used as a residence. Four of these were constructed

all around the suburbs as a reflection of the essentially ordered life of the late Victorians. The Flemington Post Office (1890, therefore strictly speaking pre-Edwardian) is truly remarkable for its elaborate decoration, not restlessly overplayed but subtly concentrated to produce a very pleasing building in the centre of an historic suburb which used to be a village on the route to Ballarat. It was designed by J.R. Brown of the Public Works. Heidelberg Court House in Jika Street was designed by J.B. Cohen at the turn of the century and constitutes the finest court house of this period. Its powerful entrance with a rubbed brick arch, its fine brickwork throughout, eaves brackets, slate roofing, cedar fittings and panelled ceiling over the court room unite to form a consistent design representative of this period.

At the other end of the scale and typical of the overplayed bad taste of the period is the Old Royal Hotel in Nelson Place, Williams town (1890), by T. Anthoness. It is a riot of Queen Anne mannerisms all run together without restraint.

The Princess May Pavilion of what is now the St Nicholas Hospital in Carlton is more restrained. It was designed by Purchas and Shields in 1901 as a red brick building on a bluestone base. Its best features are the projecting bay windows on corbels with Art Nouveau decorations.

Oakden and Ballantyne's design for the city offices of the New Zealand Loan and Mercantile Agency Company (1911), on the corner of Collins and King Streets, shows a masterly blend of brick and freestone. This is fine civic design.

Royal Hotel, Nelson Place, Williamstown. This is a face-lift designed by T. Anthoness in 1890 to an older hotel. The strongly Mannerist elevation finishes with a disturbing skyline

133

There was a bold use of steel trusses at the City Baths but much tedious and restless decoration on the outside. These were designed in 1903 by J.J. and E.J. Clark to replace the baths which had been on the site since the 1850s. The planning of these baths reflects something of the social and sexual conventions of Melbourne at that time.

> Two large swimming baths are provided, besides Turkish, vapour, slipper, and other baths. Very commodious sitting accommodation has been provided in galleries overlooking the men's swimming bath ... The slipper baths are all of American porcelain. Kosher baths are provided below for Jewish citizens, and the entrances are so planned as to make for economic administration.[15]

In 1912 there were plenty of broad acres to be possessed and built on, for the suburban 'sprawl' had hardly begun. In Collingwood there were 30.1 persons to the acre, while in Camberwell the figure was still only 1.5.[16] One of the characteristic features of the first part of this century was the development of the outer suburbs. More than this, Melbourne people were very conscious of the country and of the importance of primary industry. City architects were designing houses for country properties. Klingender and Alsop designed a pisé house for the Riverina. Australia still had some leisurely years before industrialization.

Queen Victoria's reign had been predominantly one of peace. When there was a war the involvement and the patriotism on the part of Australians was immense. This

Queensland Building, 84 William Street (1913), architects Butler and Hall. A close-up of carving around the entrance. This is a city building with Queen Anne mannerisms on a facade of Barrabool Hills stone. Note the native Australian theme in the carving. The building shows the influence of Norman Shaw with whom Walter Butler was associated

was the case with the Boer War, but even more so with the First World War, which was such a traumatic event that most of the nation's resources were diverted into the war effort. This war, followed by the Depression, meant that for the next few years there was little architecture worth speaking of.

City Baths, Swanston Street (1903), designed by J.J. and E.J. Clark. This building is a combination of simple engineering internally and rather fussy elevations externally. This could be said of much Edwardian work

During the First World War building slackened off almost to a standstill, so that the Melbourne of 1919 looked very similar to that of 1914. In every other respect there was change. The war had cost the British Empire a million lives lost outright and a million others permanently injured. Britain, bled white of money and manpower, could never again invest in Australia as she had done in the 1880s. Socially, life had changed with the emancipation of women. Spiritually, the complacency of Edwardian society and beliefs had been shattered. It was to this changed climate that the men of the A.I.F. returned.

Among them were Arthur Stephenson and Leighton Irwin. Both had remained in London for a year to study at the Architectural Association School and returned to Australia in 1920 to make their impact on the architecture of the post-war period. Arthur (later Sir Arthur) Stephenson set up practice with Percy Meldrum and made it his ambition to upgrade the architecture of Australia's hospitals.

The most recent hospital had been the Melbourne Hospital's main block fronting Lonsdale Street (now the Queen Victoria Hospital). Designed by J.J. and E.J. Clark, as the winning entry in a competition in which George Sydney Jones of New South Wales was a competitor, this building was begun in 1910. It incorporated the traditional Nightingale ward layout, with operating theatres, but little improvement on the grouping of ablution facilities in sanitary annexes. After 1920, however, fresh thought from America influenced the plan-

136

Chapter 7

Melbourne between the Wars

His helmet now shall make a hive for bees,
And, lovers' sonnets turn'd to holy psalms,
A man-at-arms must now serve on his knees,
And feed on prayers, which are age his alms.
George Peele, *Ib. Polyhymnia, Sonnet ad finem, A Farewell to Arms*

ning of hospitals, highlighting the patients' need for greater privacy and the staff's need for a higher standard of equipment.

Stephenson's first contribution to Melbourne's hospital architecture was the laundry at the old Children's Hospital (now St Nicholas Hospital) in Drummond Street. In 1927 he visited America, where hospital design was years ahead of the rest of the world. Realizing the inflexibility of load-bearing walls, he designed the Children's

Hospital outpatients' building on Rathdowne Street as the first framed hospital building in Melbourne. He engaged Fred Atherton to make sterilizers and other hospital hardware to conform to American standards. Further, his design for the Jessie McPherson Building of what is now the Peter MacCallum Clinic (1929) put into practice the idea of grouping services such as sterile supply, for economy and efficiency.

Concrete was generally accepted in the 1920s. The Surrey Hills water tower (1928) and many city buildings were constructed in reinforced concrete, but the technology about this was only just developing and there were some costly failures due to poor mixing and the insufficiency of tamping or vibrating methods. On 24 April 1925 the Tobacco Company building in Swanston Street (now part of the Royal Melbourne Institute of Technology) collapsed due to inadequately mixed concrete and the architect responsible for the design and supervision, Harold Stainsby, never overcame his remorse. Other failures only became apparent over the years due to insufficient cover for the reinforcement.

It was the possibilities of this material and the worldwide influence of Alvar Aalto of Finland which altered the external appearance of hospitals and other buildings, introducing the clean horizontal lines of external balconies. This can be seen as an uncompromising feature in Stephenson's hospital designs, including Frankston Orthopaedic (1930) with its open-air wards, St Vincent's in 1933, the Mercy Hospital in 1934, the Freemasons' Hospital in 1936,

137

*Freemasons' Hospital, East Melbourne (1936),
architects Stephenson and Meldrum. This building
with its uncompromising horizontality and sweeping
balconies clearly shows the new feeling in hospital
design and the influence of the International Modern
Movement from Europe*

and culminating in the Royal Melbourne (1939-43), which was not ready for public use until after the Second World War.

Other architects were struggling out of the Depression and finding work. The Alfred Hospital Centre Block (1938) was designed by A. and K. Henderson and the Women's Hospital laundry, kitchen and boiler house (1939) were designed by Leighton Irwin. He also produced St George's Hospital, Kew, with a quiet Georgian feeling (1936) and Prince Henry's Hospital (1940). His Heidelberg Repatriation Hospital was built during the War (1942).

In all this work just before the War it was the patient who ultimately benefited. In public wards the beds were grouped in fours and arranged parallel to the window wall and single rooms allowed for the isolation of the acutely ill. Mechanical ventilation was improving, but the cost of air-conditioning in those days placed it beyond the range of hospitals. The ward blocks therefore were long and narrow to promote cross ventilation.

These buildings belong to the 1930s. They show a strength of line and massing, plain wall surfaces and a predominating horizontality broken by a contrasting vertical feature, usually the stairwell. This is seen on a small scale in the Women's Hospital Pathology Building in Swanston Street (1938) and on a larger scale in the Royal Melbourne, where the tower is finished with a fine sensitivity. This trend is seen in other buildings of the period, notably Mitchell House, 358 Lonsdale Street (1936-37) by

139

The Royal Melbourne Hospital (1939-43). The end
wall of one of the wings shows, on the left, the
rounded concrete balconies which run the full length
of the north wall. Good brickwork and fine detailing
by John Fisher of Stephenson and Meldrum, later
Stephenson and Turner, make this building one of the
best examples of hospital architecture of the 1930s

Harry Norris; the Russell Street Police Headquarters (1940-42) by the Public Works Department (Percy Everett); and the Sanitarium Factory at Warburton by Edward Billson (1936).

Leighton Irwin's most significant contribution was in architectural education. He was director of the Melbourne University Architectural Atelier, a three-year design course, and chairman of the Board of Architectural Education. In such a position he and men like Anketell Henderson influenced all who sought a degree in architecture; in a young nation striving for national feeling and an indigenous expression in the arts there was much to teach. In 1932-33 the syllabus for architectural training was revised and modernized. The modern movement was growing in strength. Australian architects were travelling overseas and being influenced by Europe and America.

Walter Burley Griffin came to Australia in 1913 to supervise the development of Canberra. His experience on the capital was a story of frustration by officialdom. Indeed, it was this antipathy to bureaucracy and the rulebook which was a problem throughout his career in Australia. One of his neighbours in Heidelberg commented that 'he was always fighting someone'. He was a persistent positive thinker whose convictions could not be overruled. Griffin's letter-head introduced him to his Melbourne clientele as 'landscape architect', which described his work well. He possessed an awareness of the broad pattern, which included streets, trees, planting and a poetic

140

Mitchell House, 358 Lonsdale Street (1936), architect Harry Norris. This building is a good example of the European Modern Movement (in fact the first example in the city) but, apart from deterioration, there has been a lack of sensitive detailing, for instance on the corner windows

reverence for the possibilities of a site. The house was only one element in a man-made landscape and to him town-planning, sociology and landscape architecture were integral.

Griffin had already practised in Chicago where the pace quickened in the 1880s to serve a booming West and Mid-West. He had been strongly influenced by Louis Sullivan, some of whose buildings were being constructed when Griffin was a student. Sullivan in his turn had been influenced by Henry Hobson Richardson, who remembered the great granite warehouses being erected along the Boston wharves.

Sullivan had begun to eliminate classical detail and traditional forms and to replace them with pure architectural geometry. Norman Shaw and Philip Webb in England, Charles Rennie Mackintosh in Scotland and Richardson in America were delving into regional history and discovering a new vernacular style using local materials. The American movement came to fruition in Frank Lloyd Wright's philosophy of home design, culminating in his prairie houses in the first decade of this century, out of which came most of the ideas that characterize the modern American home. Griffin was a product of the Prairie School of Architecture, having worked with Frank Lloyd Wright during the innovative years of 1901-05.

In Melbourne Griffin gathered round him a small staff of dedicated people who shared his views and caught his enthusiasm. To begin with this team consisted of his wife, Marion Mahony; George Elgh, a

Chicago draftsman who had worked on the Canberra plans with Griffin; Roy A. Lippincott; Edward Fielder Billson and a stenographer. This was the complete staff for such major works as Newman College, Australia Cafe and the Capitol Theatre plus sundry plans for Leeton, Griffith, Ranelagh and other estate layouts. The pay was small and the hours were long. Griffin had no sense of time or money. Billson remembers working every night until eleven o'clock. 'In those days', he recollects, 'we used to work until we felt hungry'.

Presentation was important, although Griffin did few of the drawings himself. Presentation drawings were printed on silk and lightly tinted with dyes. His wife, Marion, a fine draftswoman, did much of the work on the Capitol Theatre ceiling, with the help of models. Griffin set up a practice first in Goode House in Collins Street, then in St Kilda Road, an 'out-of-town' address on the site of the present Bates, Smart and McCutcheon's office, and finally in Leonard House in Elizabeth Street (now demolished).

141

18 Willis Street, North Balwyn (1920); architect Eric Nicholls, who built this house for himself while a partner of Walter Burley Griffin. With its powerful horizontality, its repetitive abstract ornament, and its rugged masonry, few houses outside America show more clearly the characteristics of the style of Frank Lloyd Wright

Leslie Grant in a personal reminiscence remembers him as a man in love with life; courteous, gentle and a delight to work with. Griffin loved music and botany. On walks in the Botanic Gardens at lunchtime, he would point out a tree or a shrub ideal for such and such a landscaping situation.

Griffin believed that every man should have resource to a simple and economic method of constructing his own house. This led to the 'Knitlock' system. For a year Billson worked in close co-operation with Malcolm Moore, the engineer who designed the manufacturing plant for the system and later established the engineering company Malcolm Moore Industries. It was a modular system for constructing houses with walls 2½ inches (6.3 centimetres) thick, strengthened with piers. There were air ducts in the interlocking keys and gas and electric conductors were concealed in the chases. Griffin referred to this as 'segmental construction'.

> Segmental construction, by eliminating the extra cost of outside walls, of wings, angles and bays and buttresses, of openings for doors and windows and cupboards, through eliminating cutting and fitting, plumbing and aligning, makes possible the convenience and beauty and infinite variety within the limits of expense of our commonplace boxes or more or less dark cells which we've been driven to by sheer necessity.[1]

Hamilton Moore was also interested in the idea of cheap homes. He started a company and built a number of homes in Melbourne and Sydney.

Billson, the first diplomate in architecture from Melbourne University, left the Griffin office in 1922 when he and Lippincott won the competition for Auckland University. It was during the time he was working with Griffin that Billson, in collaboration with A.J. Smith, an engineer, drafted the first Architects' Registration Act. His father, who was a member of Parliament for thirty years, presented it unsuccessfully as a Private Member's Bill. The Act was finally passed under Kingsley Henderson in 1923. After Billson and Lippincott had left, fresh blood was brought into the office in the form of Eric Nicholls, Henry Pynor and Leslie Grant. Griffin did take on one articled pupil, J.F.W. Ballantyne.

After Griffin had laid out the Glenard Estate in Eaglemont (1916-23), Lippincott bought two blocks and built a house on one of them, 21 Glenard Drive (1917, a house which shows undoubted Griffin influence), and Griffin designed a 'doll's house' on the block next door for the Lippincott children (1919). For this he used Knitlock, and although it was only 21 feet (6.4 metres) square, he and his wife later lived in it. At that time the regulation height for a ceiling was 10 feet (3 metres) and these ceiling rafters sprang from a height of just over 6 feet 6 inches (2 metres). The building surveyor remonstrated; Griffin invited him in to listen to some music. There were ugly threats of eviction and demolition, but Griffin held his ground saying, 'Would you object if I erected a tent in the garden and lived in that?' The plea was unanswerable and the Griffins were left in occupation. (Two similar houses, the Gumnuts, were built on Oliver's Hill, Frankston in 1922.) Griffin's positive thinking frequently ran foul of the by-laws. Billson recalls saying to him, 'But this idea is contrary to the by-laws', and he replied, 'Then we must change the by-laws!' and in many cases he did just that.

After the Griffins left Melbourne the 'doll's house' at 23 Glenard Drive was unsaleable. Plaisted and Warner were commissioned to add to it to make it conform to the minimum area prescribed by the Heidelberg regulations. The original structure is still there, unseen from the street.

Work on Leonard House in Elizabeth Street was stimulating, as Burley Griffin's staff were conscious of breaking new ground in office building design. In contrast to the conventional city buildings of the day, this had a circular lift, a 'curtain wall', and a balustrade design for the main stairway which extended the full height of the building. There were also male and female rest rooms and other luxuries which were innovative at that time. It was built on a shoestring in 1923-24 for Nisson Leonard-Kanewsky, who held the agency for Kernerator Incinerators. He persuaded a number of municipalities to invest in these destructor plants, and through him Griffin was engaged as architect. The incinerator buildings were to Griffin's design, each one refreshingly original. They are to be found in other state capitals but the only one still remaining in the Melbourne area is that in Holmes Road, Moonee Ponds (1929-30).

One of his earliest jobs (1916) was Newman College at Melbourne University. He adopted a plan consisting of residential arms enclosing courtyards and meeting at two rotundas, one at each end of the site. Only half the plan was built and only one rotunda (the refectory). Regrettably, a model showing the complete scheme has been lost. Only a photograph of it remains. The refectory is enclosed by a pattern of ribbed vaulting and, with its subtle display of high-level lighting and galleries, is a brilliant example of enclosed space, a sort of miniature of the banking chamber in the C.B.A. head office in Collins Street.

> Touched with faint light, the Sullivan-inspired ornamentation literally sparkles in the mist. Below the balcony the dark-stained wood of the dining tables, doors and floor give one a sense of floating in the soft blue-white cloud of the dome.[2]

The sandstone from the Barrabool Hills is in places rough-hewn in contrast with the smooth dressing stones round the windows. The whole concept is superbly original, although we can conjecture about the various influences in the shadows of Griffin's mind—Bertram Goodhue, Anatole de Baudot, Arthur Sullivan, and so on.

He disliked the current trend, especially in 'bungalow' types, of clumsy roof shapes incorporating sleepouts. He advocated wide overhangs, flat roof shapes and the incorporation of native flora. 'Elimination of these snowshed pitches or stuffy attic quarters', he said, 'leaves a terrace for

143

Leonard House, 44-46 Elizabeth Street (1924-25, since demolished); architect Walter Burley Griffin, who had his third Melbourne office here. In its day this was a 'prestige' office building with many original features like a circular lift, rest rooms for both sexes on the top floor and a curtain wall on the front facade

outlook, for secure and airy sleepouts, and for promenade and garden'.[3]

Bill Thomas, whose father was the quarry-master supplying sandstone at Willoughby for the Castlecrag (N.S.W.) building programme, remembers working for Griffin, whose office was in one of the completed houses. Those were exciting days when Kingsford Smith flew in from America and the two arms of the Sydney Harbour Bridge were about to meet overhead. But the local council was unexciting in its demands for traditional floors built clear of the ground. In all his houses Griffin insisted on concrete slabs, pouring them first and arguing about them later. In such ways he was always fighting officialdom, but with his employees he was fair and tolerant rather than generous.

As with all his houses, there were defects. The flat roofs with their internal gutters tended to leak, and Griffin would look up at the leak and express the hope that it would mend itself. Fireplaces too were suspect and, unlike those of Frank Lloyd Wright, were not the main 'pivot' round which the house was planned. Doors to bathrooms were a foot clear of the floor, and for the traditionally minded this was too much for privacy. The strength of his work lay in its relatedness to its environment. When the masonry was finished, with all its little projections and recesses, he would go round the walls planting little bits of moss or lichen, encouraging them to spread.

Few of Griffin's Knitlock houses remain: 52 Darebin Street, Heidelberg (1920s), 16 Glyndebourne Crescent, Toorak (c.1925), and 7 Warwick Avenue, Surrey Hills (1920s), are still inhabited; 45 Outlook Drive, Heidelberg (1914), was built on a U plan with more traditional materials and is enclosed and mature in the landscaping. 88, Pleasant Road, Hawthorn (1923), is unusual in its pergola over a paved entrance court. The Lyddy factory in Fitzroy Street, Fitzroy, has been linked with the name of Eric Nicholls. There was an associate agreement enabling staff members to take on private work on a profit-sharing arrangement and this can cause confusion about the actual authorship of some jobs. Griffin's oriental patterned facade to 109 Little Bourke Street (1915) more or less remains, though it has been substantially stripped, but the building in which he excelled in his ability to handle internal space was the Capitol Theatre in Swanston Street (1924).

In the world of public entertainment the age of the motion picture had begun in Los Angeles in 1902. In Britain films were shown in Victorian theatres and music halls. The talkie had arrived in the 1920s and 300 cinemas were built in London alone.[4] The picture palace had become the temple of the motion picture and the cathedral of public entertainment. The early buildings were hardly affected by the modern movement and were produced in an historical style, providing one of the 'cultural' aspects of going to the pictures. Internally they were gorgeously decorated through the magic of fibrous plaster. The public would revel in the visual display of costly beauty, watching the soft folds of curtain after curtain slide across the proscenium opening, bathed in amber footlights.

Such was the Capitol. Although much has been made of the ceiling—'vaulted and fretted with cubes of brilliant white plaster, through which poured from 6000 concealed lamps a constant flood of coloured brilliance ...'[5] (which incidentally was entirely successful acoustically)—it was the entrance foyer and lobbies which showed spatial delight. The entrance is now remodelled but the staircase lobbies are still there. The unusual feature of the theatre was the fact that there was no proscenium, or rather that it was integrated in the auditorium. The building is entirely of reinforced concrete, even the main balcony girder, the web of which is pierced for access from foyer to balcony. Griffin worked in association with Peck and Kemter on the understanding that he would be the designer, but his design for the recessed attic floor and roof garden was not realized. Instead there was a dominating cornice line like other city buildings. As with much of Griffin's work, there was an antipathy towards this building and a resentment towards his success. The first film to be shown in this threatre, *The Ten Commandments*, was about an architect whose building collapsed.

Other architects were catching up with the backlog of theatre building. The Metro Theatre in Collins Street had been built just before the First World War; toward the end of 1928, 600 men were working round the clock in three shifts on the State Theatre (now Forum) on the corner of Russell and Flinders Streets. Here in oriental magic was

144

a new concept for entertainment for the masses, transporting them into an Arabian Nights world of eastern fantasy, with a 'flirtation gallery' and a tower surmounted by a Saracenic dome of beaten copper. The auditorium was in the form of a Florentine garden under a starlit sky with cloud effects, but it has since been drastically altered. The architect was John Eberson of New York.

The following year the Athenaeum was remodelled and Oakden and Ballantyne designed Hoyt's Regent and below it the Plaza. The Regent is now stripped and deserted, but in its day it was a wonderful example of the plasterer's art. At one time there were 120 Picton Hopkins (builder's plasterers) men on the job. The chandelier, weighing one ton, the golden dome of decorated plaster, the mezzanine gallery enriched by sculpture and pictures by Quentin Sutton were components in this unique example of the Hollywood Palace Style. Its costliest treasure was its £30 000 ($60 000) Wurlitzer Organ, which was powered by a 20 horse-power electric motor.

The Palais Theatre at St Kilda, designed by H.E. White of Chicago in 1926, was also magnificent and accommodated nearly as many as the Regent (2964 seats as opposed to 3253). Griffin had remodelled the old Palais in the early 1920s, but this was burnt to the ground.

Many thoughts were turned to a worthy memorial to honour the war dead. Two returned soldiers, P.B. Hudson and J.H. Wardrop, won the competition for a Shrine of Remembrance. Before this Annear and

145

Forum Theatre, tower (1928). This detail shows the extraordinary riot of fantasy in this building, which expressed a new concept in public entertainment

Meldrum had produced a scheme for extensive replanning in this area, a truly Renaissance layout using Swanston Street as an axial line and including a shrine and a city square. The shelving of this scheme and others in the 1930s, such as the widening of Bridge Road, Richmond, was to prove very costly forty or fifty years later.

The Shrine of Remembrance, completed in 1934, was the last of those magnificent structures where the classical order of architecture, in this case the Doric order from the Parthenon, was used to produce a monumental *tour de force* with a silhouette resembling the supposed form of the Mausoleum of Halicarnassus. All the materials were Australian: granite from Tynong, sandstone lining from Redesdale, the black marble monoliths from Buchan and the freestone frieze panels in the inner shrine and marble floor from New South Wales. The modern movement was still raw and not sufficiently accepted to produce an emotive effect. But the Shrine is an uncomplicated monument. With a fine sense of scale and superb detailing it guards its treasure and speaks its message: 'Let all men know that this is holy ground'.

The height limit in the city in the twenties was a unifying influence in the cornice line. This gave to the civic architecture of Melbourne a gracious atmosphere of scale, good manners and quiet dignity. Buildings of the 1920s include Nicholas Building in Swanston Street (1926) by Harry Norris; Temple Court in Collins Street (1926) by Barlow and Hawkins; the Myer Emporium in Lonsdale Street (built in stages beginning

146

The Shrine of Remembrance, architects Hudson and Wardrop. Foundation stone laid in 1927, dedicated by the Duke of Gloucester in 1934 in the presence of three hundred thousand people. The last of the great classical monuments on which the Doric order from the Parthenon was used. It is, as the official brochure said, 'commanding, solemn, reposeful and majestic'

in 1925) by H.W. and F.B. Tompkins; and the Bank of Australasia (now A.N.Z.) in Collins Street by Anketell and Henderson. This two-storey Reed and Barnes bank building, 394 Collins Street, had been built in 1876; but now Henderson, singularly successful in solid bank jobs, added three more floors in 1929-31 with a setback on the rising facade to allow for steel-framing the whole.

A. and K. Henderson commenced the

147

Left: Sculpture by Paul Montford and external facing in granite from Tynong

new T. and G. Head Office on the corner of Collins and Russell Streets in 1928 and finished it at the permitted height with a prominent cornice. They extended this on the Collins Street front after the company had acquired more land and, in 1936-37, completed the composition with a wedding-cake tower. Two pieces of mechanical equipment were significant at the time: a high-speed circular lift and, installed below the words 'better than to squander life's gifts is to conserve them and ensure a fearless future', a set of automatic doors activated by breaking a beam of light. For the next forty years these doors were to tax the resources and patience of the maintenance company (Brooks Robinson).

Rodney Alsop who joined A. and K. Henderson as a partner in 1921 proposed that all T. and G. buildings wherever possible should be the same colour and have a tower to identify them. While abroad he had been much influenced by the surface treatment in texture and colour of buildings around the Mediterranean, where light and climate are similar to Australian conditions. His work had a characteristic simplicity and sensitivity. He could use simple and unusual materials to obtain interesting effects.

Alsop and Conrad Sayce will always be remembered as the designers of Winthrop Hall in the University of Western Australia in 1930-32, but Melbourne also retains monuments to Alsop's creativity. St Mark's Church of England, Camberwell (1920), has a rare beauty. In the chancel it has sandstone taken from a Melbourne bank, windows by Napier Waller, and a stone relic

148

Alcaston House, Spring Street (1930), architects A. and K. Henderson. This stone-faced building for professional suites is an exercise in classical fenestration and shows a sensitive balance of surfaces, solids and voids, with balconies providing a lighter touch

from Lincoln Cathedral in the nave wall. Winster (1925) in Tintern Crescent, Toorak, is a house which shows Alsop a master of spatial relationships. The entrance vestibule, with its low intersecting barrel vault, leads into a fine stair hall enriched with Spanish decoration. The house with all its rare detailing breathes a Mediterranean atmosphere, its loggia giving access to a private and secluded garden. His final and short-lived partnership was with Bramwell Smith, who built many flats. Alsop died in 1932.

Godfrey and Spowers designed Kelvin Hall in Collins Place in 1927 as the headquarters of the Victorian Institute of Architects, and this building was converted to the Playbox Theatre in 1969. The 1930s opened with the building of Henderson's Alcaston House on the corner of Collins and Spring Streets, containing high-class professional suites, while at the other end of Collins Street two significant contracts went ahead. The former A.M.P. Society headquarters (now the Bank of New South Wales) on the corner of Collins and Market Streets and the Port Authority Building, just down the hill in Market Street, both won Royal Victorian Institute of Architects Street Architecture medals, the first in 1932 and the second in 1933. As a direct result of the 2-chain (20 metres) height limit, these buildings are almost cubic in form.

The A.M.P. Building was designed by Bates, Smart and McCutcheon and occupies the site of John Pascoe Fawkner's two-storey brick building which was used as the Melbourne Club. The Collins and Market Street facades of the building are faced with

Port Authority Building, Market Street (1929). Designed by Sydney Smith, Ogg and Serpell, this building makes a powerful visual impact with the giant Ionic order. This could never happen today, nor would we have the craftsmen to do it, but in those days such buildings added a classical elegance to Melbourne

Sydney freestone and Casterton granite. The main ground floor chamber was a large space spanned by beams 60 feet (18 metres) long. The heating was by radiant panels, whereby heating coils were concealed behind the plasterwork of the ceilings. Ventilation was by the 'Plenum' method, and there was an unusual system of external blinds. These were the latest mechanical developments in Australia, but in neither this nor the Port Authority Building was there full air-conditioning.

The Port Authority Building (1929) stands on a portion of the site of the original Customs House. It was designed by Sydney Smith, Ogg and Serpell and is significant for its four magnificent elevations featuring the giant Ionic order. Although this is a revival of a past style it is in fact a unified cubic mass, beautifully modelled according to the disciplines imposed by classical architecture in the traditional materials of granite, freestone and bronze.

The transformation on the corner of Collins and Swanston Streets (Drew's Corner) took place in 1932 as Marcus Barlow created the Manchester Unity Building, a design with the same feeling as the American Radiator Company building in New York by Raymond Hood. The building is reinforced concrete faced with faience on a vertical pattern and finished internally with fine marble and bronze detailing. It was the extensive use of faience as a facing which made this building interesting. It rose in eleven months. Barlow followed this up just before the Second World War with the faience-faced Century Building (1938-39),

150

Manchester Unity Building, corner Collins and Swanston Streets, detail of corner lantern (1932), architect Marcus Barlow. This steel-framed building is finished with faience facing tiles and superb detailing. This and Century Building, by the same architect, are the notable examples of faience work in the city

also in Swanston Street (corner of Little Collins Street). At the same time Stephenson and Turner were building the E.S. & A. Royal Bank Branch (now A.N.Z.) on the corner of Collins and Elizabeth Streets. This building was not only designed to 'look' nice, but had well designed mechanical equipment in the plant area. In fact this and the Century Building were the first air-conditioned buildings in Melbourne. (In the bank building *full* air-conditioning was restricted to certain floors.) The Provident Life Building in Queen Street (1938) had air-conditioning allowed for at a future date.

It is impossible to overrate the influence of the architects who travelled overseas in the 1930s. Following the Depression when there was little building activity, many did travel, and discovered the work of the *avant-garde* in Britain who were liberated from Edwardianism and traditional attitudes and experiencing the thrills of the 'new architecture'. This modern movement arose from the spirit of the times and out of a fusion of the technology of steel and glass, new forms of vision, an impatience with historical styles and a strong link with social needs.

Wells Coates and Maxwell Fry in Britain were concerned about the condition of the working classes and aware of the potential in the advances in technology and communication. They were joined by those architects who chose to escape from Nazi Germany, among them Marcel Breuer, Moholy-Nagy and Walter Gropius, and this confluence of brilliant minds resulted in an ar-

Century Building, corner Swanston and Little Collins Streets. Designed by Marcus Barlow just before the Second World War. There is something uncompromisingly modern in the clean vertical lines of this faience-covered building. Further, it was fully air-conditioned

151

chitectural renaissance which brought the England of the 1930s to the forefront in what is now called the 'International Modern' style. It was international in the same sense that Gothic was international, being a universally recognized way of building. Its early devotees aimed at freedom from historical connotations and attempted to make the movement 'non-stylistic', but today we have come to see the importance of historical roots and look for a message in a building design. We look back on International Modern as the 'style' of the 1930s.

Australian architects saw all this as heady stuff and returned with new vision. They could no longer follow traditional patterns. For them it was an entirely new ball game and from now on they designed with steel and concrete, long horizontal windows, balconies, flat roofs and roof gardens.

But Melbourne was a conservative city and at first the new dynamic was expressed in a pronounced verticality, as seen in Smith, Ogg and Serpell's Strand Building in Elizabeth Street (1928, now demolished) and the Myer Emporium in Bourke Street by H.W. and F.B. Tompkins (1933-35), but this style was always restricted by the city height limit. Furthermore, conservatism was expressed in some buildings with more serious associations, like the strongly Georgian Anzac House at the top end of Collins Street (Stanley Parkes, 1937) and the Royal Australian College of Surgeons in Spring Street (1936) by Leighton Irwin. Leslie Perrott's Chevron Hotel in St Kilda Road (1934) was still pleasantly Georgian.

152

Myer Emporium, Lonsdale Street (1925-26, extended 1929-35), architect Harry Tompkins. The influence of American commercial architecture can be felt in this eleven-storey emporium. The prominent cornice finished the building at a height of two chains from street level, the height limit in those days

Notable modern work in Collins Street included Newspaper House (247-249, Stephenson and Meldrum, 1932) and Kodak House (250, Oakley and Parkes, 1935). More striking still was the McPherson's building (now Board of Works, 546, Reid, Pearson and Stuart Calder, 1936), with its columns set behind continuous horizontal bands of clear glass, opal glass and Wunderlich's terra cotta. With similar feeling the Hotel Australia was designed by Leslie Perrott and Phosphate House (515) by Oakley and Parkes, both just before the Second World War.

Modern work in Bourke Street included Dunklings, since drastically remodelled (H.W. and F.B. Tompkins, 1936); Barnett's Building (164, Seabrook and Fildes, 1937), since altered by the H.B.A.; and Coles Building (299-307, Harry Norris, 1937). In Queen Street we find the Provident Life Building (A.S. and R.A. Eggleston, 1938), where the front projecting piers are not structural but merely provide a strong vertical emphasis; and Victoria House (Gawler and Drummond, 1938), again with a strong vertical emphasis.

Further, there was Yule House in Little Collins Street (Oakley and Parkes, 1933) and M.U. Oddfellows Building, now Jensen House, at 339 Swanston Street (Marcus Barlow and Associates, 1941). But the north and west elevations of this building are now exposed, due to the development of the new Museum Station and this has caused a problem. These elevations were never meant to be as prominent as the street frontage and therefore are not 'presentable'. Architects

were still wedded to the idea of 'facadism'.

However, modern architecture was generally accepted and flat roofs with all their problems were all the vogue. Even some advertisements of those days seemed to link flat roofs with the new age of aviation, suggesting no doubt the possibility of landing on roofs.

Bates, Smart and McCutcheon won the 1934 Street Architecture Award with Buckley and Nunn's new premises, 294 Bourke Street, a four-storey building clad in black terra cotta to surround a huge central glazed panel. The design featured stainless steel windows and polychrome terra cotta panels and, like Leonard House, foreshadowed the curtain wall. It brought to the street, in the words of the jury, 'a welcome note of colour, sparingly and judiciously employed'.

153

Dulverton, 379 Toorak Road (1923). This and Langi (579 Toorak Road) were two-storey blocks of flats designed by Walter Burley Griffin. Each flat is carefully designed from the point of view of internal space, and the stairs to the upper flats are 'introduced' to the building at half-landing level

In this inter-war period flats became a profitable field for investment. Griffin had produced Langi and Dulverton in the Toorak Road of the 1920s, modest two-storey blocks with a simple arrangement of external staircases disappearing inside at half-landing level. By the early thirties Arthur Plaisted was producing flats in Tudor and Keith Cheetham and Bramwell Smith were designing them in Georgian, while Marsh and Michaelson were building 'English Homes', as they were called, along St Kilda Road. Early Examples of 'modern' flats were produced, such as those in Cowderoy Street, St Kilda, by Mewton and Grounds (1936); and those in Toorak Road, South Yarra, by Scarborough, Robertson and Love (1939).

There was something of a renaissance in fine brickwork during this period. Edward Billson found a pile of underburnt and multicoloured bricks in a brickyard, bought them for half price, and used them in houses and flats in Toorak and in Walsh Street, South Yarra. These caused much interest. Robert Hamilton similarly discovered a new value for overburnt clinkers. Plaisted and Warner also used clinkers with good effect and all this led to a deeper appreciation of brickwork for its own sake. Brickyards turned out a wider range of products, including what became known as the Tapestry Brick, as used on the facing of the Littlejohn Memorial Chapel at Scotch College. Stephenson and Meldrum's front to St Vincent's Hospital (1934) is a fine exercise in the use of Wunderlich face bricks and terra cotta.

Best Overend wrote about the 'Minimum Flat' for the single working person. He had gained experience in London, first with Wells Coates and then with Serge Chermayeff, Raymond McGrath and Eric Mendelsohn. On his return in 1935 and under the name H. Vivian Taylor, Soilleux and Overend, he designed Cairo, a U-shaped block of two-storey bachelor flats in Nicholson Street, Fitzroy. These were derived from Wells Coates's Lawn Road Flats in Hampstead (1933-34), designed to meet the need of the single worker. The communal diningroom at Cairo has fallen into disuse, the concrete is spalling off exposed edges of awnings and cantilevered external staircases and the flat Malthoid roof has given a lot of trouble, yet it still remains a highly successful and well designed block of flats. Its serious deficiency is the lack of car parking space.

John Scarborough, of Scarborough, Robertson and Love, was producing a modern 'Gothic'. During his experience overseas he was influenced by, amongst others, Bertram Goodhue in the United States, and on his return won the competition for the Littlejohn Memorial Chapel at Scotch College (1936) which shows strong Goodhue influence. Similar influence is felt at St Monica's, Essendon, by Payne and Dale (1937). Louis Williams, of North and Williams, was a sensitive designer in Gothic freestyle and his work can be seen at Trinity College in the University of Melbourne and in many churches. To highlight one, the Balwyn Road Uniting Church in Canterbury (1929) is beautifully controlled by its

tower, and the progression from small vestibule into the church shows a superb handling of space. Simple shapes, plain surfaces, subtle use of clinkers and a huge hammer-beam roof spanning at the crossing 43 feet (over 12½ metres) make this a most impressive church. Significant modern work was done by Yuncken and Freeman, in spite of the depression of the early thirties. As previously mentioned, Mewton and Grounds, 'with their clean, pure, and intensely warm buildings, set Melbourne architecture alight for a brief five years'.[7]

Frederick Romberg came to Australia in 1938 and found work as a draftsman with Stephenson and Turner. Going into partnership with Richard Hocking and Mary Turner Shaw, he achieved recognition in his first private job, the Newburn Flats in Queen's Road, South Melbourne (1939). His design revealed the influence of Le Corbusier and Alvar Aalto and summed up his early training in Europe. Developing the Cairo idea, he aimed to express the privacy and individuality of each flat. To do this he broke up the block with balconies and yellow sun-blinds. He used off-form concrete extensively, with square metal plates as formwork. Innovative techniques led to on-site supervision which taxed the resources of Mary Shaw. It led to other blocks of flats in the hard war years, such as 44 Walsh Street, South Yarra (1941), and eventually, in the fifties, to that brilliant association of creative minds, Grounds, Romberg and Boyd.

In the field of education Ray Davey in the Public Works Department designed the

Newburn Flats, Queens Road, South Melbourne (1939-40). Designed by Frederick Romberg, this block of flats overlooking the park had many new features. There was a measure of privacy for each flat, and concrete off steel formwork was used with very clean effect

Melbourne Boys High School (1927) like a Tudor collegiate building and, by contrast, Norman Seabrook (Seabrook and Fildes) made a vital contribution to the modern movement of the early 1930s by designing the MacRobertson Girls' High School (1934). In this fine brick building we have the first modern school. Its lines are predominantly horizontal and each element in the composition—classroom, stairwell, gymnasium—is an honest expression of its function. Seabrook and Fildes did much modern work of significance.

During the Depression, when millions were jobless and homeless, the yearning for a home of one's own was one of the most powerful of motivations in capitalist societies. This was so of Australia, where the average person preferred to live in his own house surrounded by freehold land and, since the last home-building period in Edwardian days, many improvements had come.

For the structure, Cindcrete Blocks were available as an alternative to brick or brick veneer or, for cheaper houses, Hardie's fibro-cement on a timber frame. By 1922 ceiling heights were being reduced to 11 feet (3.3 metres) and even to ten feet (3 metres), but flat roofs were a constant source of trouble. Before the days of metal decking the built-up bituminous roof would fare badly in excessive heat or wet. In fact when Geoffrey Mewton designed a house with a flat roof at 72 Halifax Street, Brighton, in 1936 the owner found it difficult to raise finance due to prejudice on the part of the bank.

156

Yarrabee, 44 Walsh Street, South Yarra (1941). The architect, Frederick Romberg, intended this block of flats to be painted white and lifted off the ground on 'pilotis' (Le Corbusier's word for stilts or columns). However, economies made compromise inevitable. The formwork to the concrete balconies was corrugated iron, but even after the passage of time the building still looks clean and 'modern'

Labour-saving devices were adding to the convenience of a home. 'Oil-o-matic' heating, for instance, was available for the expensive home and the 'Comet' spray bath and fuel bath heater were being advertised as the latest in bathroom comforts. By 1927 Hecla were advertising a variety of electric appliances and Brooks Robinson were pushing 'Luxfer' glazing and parquetry flooring. By 1933 'Feltex' was available for floor coverings; by 1937 Everhot were in business for hot water and a Sunshine exhaust fan could remove the fumes from a kitchen. In 1910 Robert Wardrop, a New Zealander, experimented with a mixture of plaster and flax and produced plaster sheet; and by 1930 all lath-and-plaster wall and ceiling lining had been superseded by fibrous plaster, later itself to be superseded by plaster board.

The double-hung sliding sash window was slowly giving way to casements and awnings and in the more expensive jobs timber windows were being replaced, in the twenties by mono-metal, in the thirties by stainless steel and after the Second World War by aluminium.

In the years between the wars most houses were constructed by builders without the services of an architect and with just enough documentation to safisfy the building surveyor. A modest house could be bought for less than £1000. Due to the many influences reaching Australia from overseas, the design of houses in this period was in a confused state, but broadly speaking we can pick out five main types:

Californian Bungalow. This house was

458 Victoria Parade, East Melbourne (1935). Three-storey flats designed by London architect I.G. Anderson. This is an example of the Art Deco fashion in architecture and decoration which was concurrent with the International Modern style of the 1930s

157

characterized by generous sweeping gables with prominent barge-boards. The eaves end of barge-boards and rafters were cut to sharp angles. Porches were deep set behind stumpy piers and dwarf walls. The finish of walls alternated between brickwork and pebble-dash. Its ground-hugging air of informality seemed to provide the returning soldier with the comfort and security he was seeking.

Spanish or Spanish Mission. This was introduced to Australia by Professor Leslie Wilkinson of Sydney in 1922. It came from California and featured colonnaded loggias, patterned render on walls, punctuated by pierced decorative panels. Sometimes barley-sugar columns were used and novel shapes on the top of pierced chimneys. Roman tiles were used on the roof. In Melbourne Dunstan and Reynolds were among the architects who used this style.

English Tudor. This arose out of English post-war romanticism and featured generous brick chimneys, Tudor half-timber work and steeply pitched roofs. Although in England it appeared in the ubiquitous semi-detached villa, here it seems to have been confined to homes for the affluent. It is seen at its best in the houses by Robert Hamilton, L.J.W. Reed and Marcus Barlow in the Toorak-South Yarra area.

Georgian. There was a specific revival of Georgian-type rectangular elevations and regularly spaced, double-hung, sliding-sash windows (though with improved methods of hanging and sliding)—a sort of hangover of eighteenth-century good taste as if nothing had changed. This again was housing for

158

Alkira House, Queen Street (1937), architect J.H. Wardrop. A rare example of Melbourne Art Deco architecture finished basically in black faience. There is a touch of industrial design here as the traditional cornice has given way to the curved, or streamlined, top

Footscray Town Hall (1936), designed by J. Plottel with careful detailing, modern in a sense, yet with some strangely Byzantine detailing in the loggia arcading. Note the variety of bricks which were available in the 1930s

the affluent. For the not-so-affluent, timber weatherboard construction of Edwardian days continued with little change.

Modern. The modern movement in home design was begun by men like Robin Dods in Queensland, George Sydney Jones in New South Wales and Harold Desbrowe Annear, Robert Haddon and Walter Burley Griffin in Melbourne, and made little headway until the thirties, when the International Modern style had some effect here. However, it would be more accurate to say that Annear, Haddon and Griffin were not specifically 'modern' architects. Each one was fresh and innovative as a designer, but also coloured somewhat by the fashion current in his day. Mewton and Grounds commenced practice in 1933 and in five years produced some brilliantly innovative houses and flats, like Clendon Flats, Cr. Malvern Road and Clendon Drive in Toorak (1940). Others took up the theme—Edward Billson, Alec Eggleston, Stuart Calder, Rhys Hopkins, Seabrook and Fildes, Best Overend and Buchan, Laird and Buchan. This work formed a conspicuous minority in a country where 90 per cent of homes were not architect-designed. However, something of the freshness of the European movement wore off as the new concept merged with the traditional Australian way of suburban building. It became confused with jazz and Art Deco forms in architecture and decoration.

Instances of Art Deco can be seen in such buildings as Lonsdale House (1930s, 269 Lonsdale Street) and 458 Victoria Parade, East Melbourne, the latter designed in 1935 by I.G. Anderson. Both have a vertical feature which finishes at the top like a pack of cards after a poor shuffle. Alkira House in Queen Street was designed in 1937 by J.H. Wardrop and is finished in grey, light green and predominently black terra cotta, its curved top in lieu of a cornice looking like a precurser of the modern radiogram.

After the great town hall-building age, town halls in the newer suburbs were designed in a variety of ways. Footscray Town Hall, designed by J. Plottel in 1936, is unique for its Byzantine detailing. The same architect designed the Beehive Building in Elizabeth Street (1934) which, with its long windows and horizontality of feeling, belongs to the modern movement. In 1934-36 Harry Johnston remodelled the old brick Richmond Town Hall with a 'classical' face-lift. Like Joseph Reed's Melbourne Town Hall, his entrance portico straddles the footpath, but less successfully. The finest modern town hall was that of Heidelberg (1937), for which the architects, Peck and Kemter, in association with Leith and Bartlett, it is believed, were inspired by the hall at Hilversum in Norway.

Up the Yarra valley, Justus Jorgensen was offered land in 1935. As an artist he had been attracted to Eltham for many years and now, following a tour of Europe and the Rhone valley in particular, he built a simple cottage of pisé (1935). The slate for the roof was given to him, a cast iron staircase was picked up from a wrecker's yard and the labour was given by his disciples, working under local tradesmen. This was the beginning of Montsalvat.

Believing that man must maintain contact with the natural environment or the fibre of life would be weakened, Jorgensen employed local tradesmen when many were out of work and he used local materials. Like William Morris, his energies were fired by the joy and satisfaction of making a thing of beauty. Ignoring historical difference in style, he blended many elements together to create a work of art, believing that architecture cannot be pigeon-holed into styles or periods, but simply into 'good' and 'bad'. John Ruskin said:

It does not matter one marble splinter whether we have an old or new architecture... The forms of architecture already known are good enough for us, and far better than any of us... A man who has the gift will take up any style that is going... and will work in that and be great in that.[8]

Surveyor Robert Hoddle set his seal on Robert Russell's preliminary work in 1837 and the town of Melbourne was planned as a rectangular grid aligned on the Yarra bank. He set out main streets a chain and a half wide (30.2 metres) and introduced small streets half a chain wide (10 metres) between them to act as access lanes, or 'mews', to the rear of the properties. The grid-iron plan consisted of a frontage to the Yarra of a mile (1.6 kilometres) and a breadth of three-quarters of a mile (1.2 kilometres) aligned on a 28° variation from true north-south. This was entirely logical. Melbourne was sited just below the falls at a point on the Yarra where ships could pull in and its alignment was dictated by the direction of the course of the river there. Its extent was restricted by the hills to the east and west and such a grid layout could conveniently be drained by Williams Creek.

So the boundaries of the town were from the Yarra by Spring, Latrobe and Spencer Streets back to the river, a simple surveying exercise. This rectangular pattern was adopted for most of Victoria's country towns (e.g., Ballarat West). Most colonists accepted it as a practical layout for a town in the English-speaking world. But there were disadvantages in such a grid-iron development which took little account of physical variation or contours and allowed neither for crescents nor squares as in the great eighteenth-century towns. Furthermore, 'the streets betray their negative function as the strips between the private land by the way in which their ends are so often in trouble. One disadvantage suffered by

Chapter 8

Melbourne as a Town Plan

I...pondered how men fight and lose battle, and the thing that they fought for comes about in spite of their defeat, and when it comes turns out to be not what they meant, and other men have to fight for what they meant under another name.
William Morris

many a street was its casual emptying out into the countryside like the south-west end of Bourke Street, which petered out into a swamp, until the railways came'.[1] Natural features like the Yarra were not incorporated into the plan of the town. Planning was mean rather than noble. Public buildings were sited on street corners and not facing generous squares as in Adelaide.

The town could not be contained in a rectangle. As Garryowen said, the 'town kept

gradually pushing its way into the bush'.[2] Emerald Hill gained in attraction at the expense of Batman's Hill and Gardiner was soon to drive his bullocks out of town along what was to become Toorak Road. Hoddle more than any other guided the development of the growing town, extending his influence to Williamstown, Brighton, Geelong and other Victorian country towns. The broad streets leading out of town—St Kilda Road, City Road, Victoria Street and Royal Parade—are his work, the latter developing from the northbound bullock track later to become the Great South Road, then the Hume Highway, so that modern Melbourne has entered the motor age without actually choking. Hoddle's recommendations reveal an appreciation of ecology and he also encouraged the preservation of Aboriginal names.

Further, he was responsible for slicing up the whole suburban area into one-mile-square megablocks, and these can be traced as roads a mile (1.6 kilometres) apart, both north-south and east-west, on the street maps. This grid creates an efficient communications network but is visually mono-tonous. Some have dubbed it 'prairie planning'.

Only three years after the founding of Melbourne, Fitzroy, Collingwood and Richmond were laid out. The best areas were considered to be on the higher ground of Fitzroy and on the hill in Richmond overlooking the Yarra, while the poorer residential land was on the lower-lying flats of 'East Collingwood', as it was then called, and on the barren basalt river flats of

Burnley and Richmond. The layout seems to have been the work of individual surveyors working without a co-ordinating pattern. The owner of a Crown portion would set out the streets not according to a regional plan, but with a view to selling large allotments priced according to frontage feet and in all cases the gridiron was ideal for speculation. From the corner of Flinders and Spring Streets the alignment of Wellington Parade-Bridge Road was due east and the remainder of the suburban roads were set out east-west, north-south, except where they deviated to follow the banks of rivers. Victoria Street and Hoddle Street became the boundaries of the town reserve. The road pattern developed from Hoddle's original framework, but in most cases 'the speculator was credited with the immediate profits resulting from his operations, the long-term losses accrued to the residents and the public purse'.[3] It was all to become an enormous grid-layout sprawl.

The Building Act of 1849 referred only to the town of Melbourne and South Fitzroy and did not correct irregularities in any other suburb. Thus we find on portion 74 in East Collingwood as many as 400 building plots on 26 acres (10.5 hectares), or almost 16 per acre; a repetition of English 'by-law' planning at its worst. Removing bottlenecks and irregularities became a major theme in the local politics of the day. In 1855, for instance, there was much political discussion about an east-west ring road linking the settlement on the Maribyrnong River with the newly developed market gardens in Boroondara (Kew) and beyond,

leading to the 'battle for the Collingwood bridges'. Eventually Johnston Street became the through road.

In the layout of new suburbs topography and natural beauty seemed to set a tone and attract a class, while in other areas where unhealthy vapours resulted from overflowing cesspits, the overcrowding and lack of amenities limited the kind of visual and social environment that could develop there. In spite of the rise in real estate values resulting from the gold rush, there was a concentration of the under-privileged in some inner-suburban areas, providing a pool of cheap labour for the factories which developed there later in the century.

Richmond developed in the forties as an upper-class suburb, with its large houses and churches on Church Street Hill, where 25-acre (10 hectare) allotments were divided into 6-acre (2.4 hectare) ones. Nearer the river it became an out-of-town retreat, and the original allotment frontage in the vicinity of Barkly Gardens was 90 feet (27.4 metres). In those days the Cremorne Gardens in Richmond, constituting Melbourne's zoo and fun park, extended from Swan Street down to the Yarra. Toll was charged on the bridge leading to Hawthorn. In the 1880s the area deteriorated socially and economically, partly because of the influx of Irish immigrants and partly because of the flooding of the market with manufactured goods from Europe.

The Botanic Gardens and Domain were set aside as public reserves. Royal Park was preserved, but north of this in the Merri Creek and Clifton Hill area there were

quarry holes and the barren land did not invite immediate subdivision. South of the river the lack of a bridge retarded progress, but eventually the municipality of Emerald Hill (South Melbourne) was born and the Land Act of 1862 enabled the Albert Park area to be clearly defined. There is both noble and mean planning in South Melbourne. St Vincent's Gardens and its crescents stand out as a layout in the best Renaissance town-planning tradition, yet in 1875 there were some allotments in Raglan Street as small as 12 feet (3.7 metres) wide with no right-of-way to the rear.

Melbourne's rapid suburbanization was very British. It was regarded as a matter of pride that elegant mansions and villas were being built out of town, as the rich crossed the river to develop South Yarra, Hawthorn and Kew or even as far afield as St Kilda and Brighton, passing 'Canvastown' on the way south.

Whereas 'the rolling English drunkard made the rolling English road', the straight line was favoured for most routes in the colony. The road to Arthur's Seat ran diagonally across Brighton and the flat plain to the Mornington Peninsula. Hawdon and Burke pioneered the mail route to Yass over the Dividing Range. Gold-seekers wound their way across the marshes of the Maribyrnong and headed for Melton, Ballan and Mount Buninyong. Mount Alexander Road through the little village of Flemington was already a well-worn stock route leading north through Keilor, across the Maribyrnong, over the basalt plains, through the Black Forest to Kyneton and the Forest Creek goldfield. The route from Melbourne to Gippsland was blocked by the Koo-wee-rup Swamp and the Strzelecki Ranges, but the movement of the Overlanders after the New South Wales drought of 1838-39 eventually created watering places in the districts now known as Bayswater, Vermont and Ringwood. The stock routes from these places to Melbourne grew into the three major highways of today: Burwood Highway, Canterbury Road and Maroondah Highway.

After the discovery of gold, and in the ten years 1851 to 1861, the population of Melbourne increased five-fold to 126 000. By 1871 three-quarters of the population still lived in the city and inner suburbs.[4] At the height of the 'boom' small allotments cost more than in London and shops were rented at sums of up to £2000 ($4000) a year. During this period Melbourne acquired the character of a metropolis with some architectural pretensions. Services such as water and gas were hard pressed to keep up with the developing suburbs. The lack of Yarra bridges restricted communication from north-west to south-east. In the 1850s the first railway in Australia was built from Sandridge (Port Melbourne) to Flinders Street, but within the town the people had to be content with horse-drawn buses. Elizabeth Street would sometimes run as a strong stream and in 1858 a man and his horse were drowned in it. After a horse and dray were carried down Swanston Street into the river near the present site of Young and Jackson's, someone suggested that lifebuoys be hung along the street.

In 1851 George Wharton planned the village of Kew from Kew Junction eastwards (finishing 45 miles (73 metres) beyond Derby Street). Following Hoddle's practice, he set out the streets on a squared pattern with major and minor streets. Kew was the town of Melbourne on a smaller scale.

As described in Chapter 1, Henry Dendy's selection of 5120 acres at Brighton has left its impression on the subsequent development of that area. It was described as open forest land, timbered with gum, oak, cherry and honeysuckle, and was located five miles from the Melbourne town boundary, just missing a large patch of swampy ground at Elsternwick. Dendy was called upon to reserve the squatters' road to Arthur's Seat, already well travelled, which bisected the land diagonally. This was the only easement. (However, in those days the preferred method of transport between Melbourne and the Point Nepean Peninsula (Mornington Peninsula) was by ship, and this is how Point Nepean limestone was brought to the growing town. Later in the century bay steamers made it possible for Sorrento to grow as a popular tourist resort.)

'Marine residences' were advertised in the original subdivision. These consisted of large blocks along the shore line, quite distinct from the 'village' part of Brighton between Arthur's Seat Road and the creek bed. Brighton seemed for a while to develop accoring to income and social status, but this could not be said generally of Melbourne.

H.B. Foot's survey of Brighton of the early 1840s, the winning entry in a competition, included a 'town reserve' with a series of streets on a semi-circular pattern off a rectangular grid. Around this Foot planned a green belt of triangular areas of land. His plan for the town was a reflection of the English Regency crescents and, while residentially more pleasant than Hoddle's rectangular grids, was unusual in a new colony. It stands out as an isolated island of careful planning in a vast sea of casual suburban development.

There were over 150 properties in Foot's plan and in view of the uncertain water supply, this made an ambitious beginning to the small town. 'Surely there exists no more fitting memorial to the land boom period of the forties than the over-splendid crescents of Brighton.'[5] Apart from the town reserve and the superior blocks along the shore line, the remainder of Brighton was subdivided for cultivation into blocks ranging in size from 4 acres (1.6 hectares) to 27 acres (10.9 hectares). Later the railway cut through this street pattern, first to Bay Street and in the 1880s to the beach, the pier and the baths. At this point there is a tunnel under the esplanade linking the beach with the railway station. This was to have been an access from a ship to Brighton and Victoria—Victoria's 'front door'.

Although in many areas the railway brought efficient transport and boosted land sales, it was constructed without vertical segregation from the existing road pattern and, not conforming to the pattern, created dead-ends, dividing neighbourhood

163

units and leaving a legacy (in 1929) of 155 level crossings.[6]

The vigorous development of the times strained the lines of communication to the limit and these in their turn had a reciprocal influence, for the extension of the railway network induced people to go and live as far afield as its termini and beyond. Generally speaking the railways created their own demand. The railway station and the building of the Grand Hotel would create a centre, sometimes at the expense of another, older, centre. In Yarraville, for instance, Stephen Street was planned as the main social and shopping centre, but the opening of the Yarraville Railway Station in 1871 created a rival centre in Anderson Street, and today several empty shops in Stephen Street are witness to its decline. Further, despite the introduction of workmen's tickets, there was a discernible social distinction between those who travelled by train and those who travelled by the cable tram network. The rich tended to live in the outer areas, east of the Yarra, out of reach of the trams.

Growth was unco-ordinated and marred by local rivalry. The voices of Bent, Gilles and Berry could be heard in the local politics of the 1870s. The Hobson's Bay Railway Company was at variance with Victorian Railways and each played a mutually destructive game on the tramway's catchment area. Some acted for personal interest or to benefit his own area and the northern districts were neglected. The railways were built more from political pressures than for economic demand and nowhere was this more clearly illustrated than in the abortive 'outer circle' line which lasted three years, linking Oakleigh, Camberwell, Kew and Fairfield.

Cable trams in the 1880s were better planned, covering at first the inner suburbs and later extending their routes down St Kilda Road to Prahran, North Melbourne, West Melbourne and Port Melbourne. Horse trams were introduced on the Kew and Hawthorn routes to link up with the cable. The cable routes were interlaced with the railway lines, intersecting or touching them at eighteen points, sometimes at the suburban stations themselves.[7] Innovations like the now extinct Box Hill tramway were clearly to boost land sales in the area.

The first overseas telegraph message to be received in Melbourne in 1872 ended the appalling isolation from the rest of the world and the capture of Ned Kelly closed the era of the 'wild colonial boys'.[8] Melbourne became more civilized and the land and building boom of the eighties saw a vigorous expansion of Greater Melbourne. Between 1881 and 1891 its population increased from 284 874 to 491 700, the major part of this increase being absorbed by the newer municipalities in the relatively underdeveloped northern and western areas, such as Essendon, Flemington, Kensington, Brunswick and Footscray. There was little alteration, however, in the population density and in most suburbs the single-family, one-storey house in its own garden was the pattern. As early as 1888 the quarter-acre block was introduced and from then on the detached home on this size of block became the ideal. 'The obvious result of such largesse of private space was a suburban sprawl unrivalled anywhere but on the west coast of the United States.'[9]

In this growth there was some discrimination on the basis of social status. A guide book description of the day, for instance, rated Toorak as an 'upper-class' suburb, and those areas described by the estate agents as having a view of the bay and the bush were taken up by those who could afford them, while the less interesting river flats were inhabited by the poor. Judged by overseas standards, however, Melbourne's suburbs were remarkable for their variety, with small cottages standing beside boom-style mansions in artless co-existence.

In an Act of Parliament of 1890, the Melbourne and Metropolitan Board of Works was set up as the first overall metropolitan authority and its responsibilities were defined. It was to have control over such things as water catchment and sewerage disposal. (It did not become a town-planning authority until 1954.) This metropolitan authority was overdue. The inadequacy of the water supply lay in its reticulation rather than in any deficiency of the Yan Yean scheme, which had been in operation since the 1850s. The problem of cesspits on badly drained ground was a growing one. Night carts were emptied into the Yarra from the Johnston Street Bridge (the Penny Bridge) and other places, creating, with wool-scouring, slaughter yards and other industries, a dangerously polluted river. Outbreaks of typhoid were common. Mortality in the suburbs was

164

generally greater than in the city and greater than in London, and there was no excuse, for the population was well fed and clothed and not crowded together. The essential services (water, sewerage, gas, roads) followed in the wake of private developers but were not able to match the pace. Even in 1889 night soil was being deposited on market gardens in areas like Brighton, Footscray, Port Melbourne and Prahran; stormwater, urine and household drainage were fed into open drains and eventually flowed into the Yarra, the Maribyrnong or one of their tributaries. Unlike Sydney, Melbourne was not favoured by topography for sewerage disposal and was hampered by unco-operative local authorities. In 1887 a Royal Commission was appointed and ten years later a new sewerage scheme was in operation with an outfall at Werribee and a pumping station of opulent French Renaissance design at Newport.

Many Victorians had the vision of an ideal town. In 1889 the *Building and Engineering Journal* published a design by Phillip Treeby for Hopetown, a model suburb near Melbourne. This was a symmetrical layout with axes and crescents, but it never left the drawing board.

By the turn of the century fresh ideas from Camillo Sitte and German planners were beginning to influence town planning. *Town Planning in Practice: an Introduction to the Art of Designing Cities and Suburbs*, by Raymond Unwin, was published in 1909, recording Unwin's experience as architect/planner of New Earswick, Letchworth (begun 1903) and Hampstead Garden Suburb. Unwin attacked 'by-law architecture' which resulted from rigid specifications on layout, building heights and forms of construction, putting the case for more flexible controls and a reasoned approach to road widths. These influences affected Australia.

At this time Braybrook was a wind-swept plain consisting of a few streets running at right-angles off the Ballarat Road. An industrialist from Ballarat, Hugh Victor McKay, decided to move his plant nearer to Melbourne to save freight costs. He selected Braybrook Junction as his centre of operations because it had railway facilities within convenient distance from shipping. In so doing he showed a rare gift for planning a garden suburb. Moving his factory and personnel during 1906 and 1907, he named the place Sunshine, breathing new life into a depressed area. McKay was a Victorian of high morals and noble gestures whose life was guided by the protestant ethic of hard work, thrift and the sanctity of all human achievement.

At least 200 of his Ballarat employees followed him to Sunshine, McKay encouraging resettlement by underselling land to those prepared to build houses within a year. Repayments could be made out of wages. Although the estate is rapidly disappearing under pressure from private developers, it is significant for a number of reasons. Whereas the houses are small timber ones, typical of Ballarat at that time (one house in Sunshine is, in fact, an exact replica of a house in Lydiard Street Ballarat), the blocks are large enough to satisfy today's standards and to enable the residents to grow their own vegetables. In the layout of the estate McKay, considering the total life of man, provided parks and recreation reserves, a school, a hospital and a church.

Melbourne's parks show a variety of landscaping patterns with a mixture of native and imported trees. James Sinclair designed Fitzroy Gardens (c.1870) in the city and the Botanic Gardens were the work of William Guilfoyle. Here, with the Yarra Improvement Works of 1900-01, the old billabongs were incorporated as lakes. In these gardens we see Guilfoyle as a landscape designer *par excellence*. He uses trees almost architecturally and in a masterly way creates spaces, or grass-covered areas, leading sequentially one into another in a series of closed vistas, sometimes a tree forming a climax. As an example of Victorian landscaping the Botanic Gardens are without equal in the world. The huge range of botanical specimens reflects the first Director von Meuller's enormous energy and worldwide interest. There is an emphasis, too, on horticultural display and on bedding out. In Melbourne's moist temperate climate the gardens have reached a marvellous maturity.

The need was felt for more decisive planning, and in 1913 the Victorian Town Planning and Parks Association was formed, with responsibilities ranging over town and country for securing better housing, protecting existing parks, safeguarding native animals and erecting memorials to explorers. This later became the Town and

Country Planning Association. In the following year a conference of the Australian Natives' Association passed a resolution against slums, and stated the minimum requirements for good housing.

In 1919 a town planning conference was held to consider traffic congestion, housing deficiencies, zoning and the 'expansion and development of the metropolis on definite lines and blending the ideal with the practical'. Following complaints to the government, a further conference was held the next year and finally it was recommended to set up a commission, leading in 1922 to the Metropolitan Town Planning Commission for Greater Melbourne. The terms of reference covered the control and guidance of all future development and the preparation of estimates for improvement schemes.

Towards the end of the last century, while the Yarra valley in the Heidelberg area was inspiring Australia's first native school of painting, the man who was to make a significant contribution to town-planning in Australia and leave his mark indelibly in this area was growing and training in America. Walter Burley Griffin came to Australia as a result of winning the Canberra competition in 1911, and was appointed Director of Design and Construction for the Capital for a period of three years, with the right to private practice. He went to Sydney in 1914 and was responsible for the development of Castlecrag estate. On moving to Melbourne, he set up house in Eaglemont and designed several houses (see Chapter 7). Peter Keam commissioned Griffin to lay out the Glenard Estate at Eaglemont, and the following was exhibited on a brochure distributed at the sale:

The birth of a town planning association in Melbourne is quite a recent event, though that it was bound to come, is obvious. The Town Planning Association of Victoria considers its work a patriotic duty, arguing that we cannot afford to lag behind other parts of the world moulding the form of suburban development. The Association has been unable to persuade some municipalities to adopt minimum sized allotments for residential purposes. Mr Keam is a member of the association and he entrusted the laying out of sections of the Mount Eagle district to Mr Walter Burley Griffin (Federal Capital Designer), thus guaranteeing development on modern lines.[10]

Glenard was the first section of the Mount Eagle estate and at an auction in 1916 all the lots were sold, although no roads or footpaths had been formed. (These were made forty years later.) Glenard Drive and Mossman Drive curve pleasantly between Mount Eagle and the river. Three internal reserves were provided, two being connected, completing a figure of eight. Each reserve is entered by means of a narrow access lane 10 feet (3 metres) wide. Griffin followed this with a design for the Mount Eagle section, which is a hill with a view of the east over the Yarra valley. The layout was in the form of three concentric curved streets, each following the contours of the hill. As at Glenard, access lanes lead into three internal reserves.

Whereas fifty years earlier the native timber would have been replaced by European deciduous trees and the streets laid out in a grid-iron pattern, the streets at Eaglemont curved pleasantly through native timber, fulfilling the surveyor's nightmare and the landscape designer's dream. Griffin, of course, was influenced by the garden city movement and planned with middle or higher income groups in mind; but at Eaglemont we see a unique example of early twentieth-century town-planning in Australia. In 1928 Griffin planned two subdivisions at Keilor, incorporating curved streets but on a less propitious site. The environment near the Maribyrnong is treeless, and the development proved barren in his lifetime. (Griffin died in India in 1937.) It has recently gone ahead in a modified form. He also laid out the Ranelagh Estate at Mount Eliza.

The Metropolitan Town Planning Commission as amended in 1925 noted that 3½ acres (1.4 hectares) of Fishermen's Bend was unplanned and unoccupied except for a few small fishermen's huts. Here was the ideal site for an industrial suburb. The State Savings Bank purchased 45 acres (18 hectares) of this waste Crown land to build a bank housing scheme and the bank's architect stated that the layout 'emerged out of economical, functional necessity in planning'. The general manager, G.E. Emery, returned from a visit to England in 1926 where he had seen Welwyn and other English housing schemes.

So the first stage took place between

Williamstown Road and Howe Parade on allotments 33 by 164 feet (10 by 50 metres), each house of 13.5 squares (125 square metres) costing £886 5s. The subsoil being sea sand, pier-and-beam footings were adopted. The hollow walls were of 'Cindcrete', finished externally with coloured cement render. The name 'Garden City' was chosen to encourage residents to care for their front gardens, but any connection with the English Garden City Movement is obscure.

Following this, the Housing Commission commenced urban renewal on land immediately adjoining on the north, and by the start of the Second World War, Garden City consisted of 340 acres (138 hectares) residential and 80 acres (32 hectares) open space and playing fields. The development does have a peculiarly English appearance.

The final report of the Town Planning Commission was not published till 1929. This was a thorough and well illustrated work and in many ways prophetic. Many new road and road-widening schemes were put forward (like the widening of Sydney Road, Brunswick) which, had they been acted on then, would have saved fortunes later. But this was Depression time and nothing was done. The most far-reaching proposals were for zoning. Until then no council had had the power to prohibit houses and in most of Melbourne there was a mixture of houses, shops and factories, at the developer's whim. Minimum allotment sizes were revolutionary, namely: area A (outer suburbs), slightly less than a quarter-acre—836 square yards (697 square metres); area B, 670 square yards (558 square metres); and area C (inner suburbs), 446 square yards (372 square metres) and a frontage of not less than 35 feet (10.7 metres). The ratio of parks and playgrounds to population recommended was 5 acres (2 hectares) for each 1000 people and the development of river and creek banks for public enjoyment was proposed.

The consequences were far-reaching. 'After the Second World War Melbourne had fewer persons to the acre than in any of the great cities of the nineteenth century—only half as many as Greater London or Birmingham, a quarter as many as New York; only Los Angeles, the automobile city of the twentieth century, had lower density.'[11] The 1929 Commission reported a finding which should have been obvious to anyone:

> The cost of transport, water, sewerage, power, lighting, road construction, and maintenance generally, must fall much more heavily upon those residing in a metropolis where the density of population averages about six to the acre, as compared to a city where there are 20, 40, or more people to the acre.[12]

In 1944 the Town Planning Act empowered municipalities to produce their own plans but there was no town planning in the modern sense of that word until after the Second World War. Nowadays there are two authorities concerned with the town and country planning of the Melbourne area—the Town and Country Planning Board and the Melbourne and Metropolitan Board of Works (M.M.B.W.). In 1962-63 the population of Melbourne reached two million.

In 1954 the M.M.B.W. produced a 'trend' plan for Melbourne (as distinct from the 'intervention' plan for Sydney) and subjected its own area to land-use zoning under an Interim Development Order. Since the Second World War Melbourne has more than doubled its size and contains 20 per cent of Australia's population. It is a multi-purpose city, and because of its favourable water supply and seemingly endless countryside stretching away to the north and west has more growth potential and is therefore better fitted to accept refugees and immigrants than any other Australian city. Although at the time of writing population growth has been retarded, by the year 2000 Melbourne could have four or five million people.

Epilogue

In a short history of 146 years Melbourne has grown into one of the world's great cities. After the Second World War the building industry, being still largely traditional in outlook, climbed painfully back onto its feet and struggled with the shortage of materials. Exactly a hundred years after the gold rush Melbourne again received European immigrants by the shipload, and European tradesmen, especially the Dutch, raised the standard of trade practice here. Italians brought with them their traditional expertise in concrete and terrazzo work. In a quarter of a century a new generation of tradesmen and innovative designers have transformed Melbourne into a high-rise city of international standard.

Enormous changes have taken place in the last thirty years. Australia under the Menzies Government became an industrial nation and in many ways changed from being a nation of manual workers to a nation of businessmen. Victoria has developed light and heavy industry and Melbourne has grown (sprawled?) in an easterly, lopsided way, with residential development and shopping complexes seemingly independent of public transport networks almost to the Dandenongs. So much so that the pattern of Melbourne today reinforces the necessity for private transport. The fruit orchards and market gardening of Templestowe and Doncaster have disappeared for ever.

Austerity marked the first houses of the 1950s and brickwork and joinery were of a poor standard. Government controls diverted 80 per cent of resources into the construction of houses. In the developing suburbs the simple weatherboard home with corrugated asbestos roofing was sufficient at first, but the rise in affluence brought a demand for brick walls and tiled terra cotta roofs. Some municipalities even proclaimed 'brick' areas to preserve their respectability. Through such publications as *Home Beautiful*, *Women's Weekly* and the *Age Small Homes* there was no shortage of reasonable plans available to work from. The triple-fronted brick veneer with 'waterfall' windows and chimneys was popular. After 1955 modern trends in housing gained ground and the rectangular plan shapes gave way to L, T and U shapes. The skillion, or single-pitch roof, and even the butterfly, were used as variants on the pitched roof with hips or gables. There was more honesty in the use of materials.

Harry Seidler in Sydney was producing clean box-like shapes in concrete for houses, as if inspired by Le Corbusier, and architects like Frederick Romberg, Roy Grounds, Robin Boyd and Peter McIntyre were in the *avant garde* in Melbourne, the last-named using light steel framing and cladding for houses. Standard Steel were introducing open-web joists and the potential of the material was being explored by the more innovative. Aircraft hangars at Avalon were constructed in 1954 of lightweight steel spanning 276 feet (84 metres) and in the same year Mussen Mackay

and Potter designed a boiler and turbine building at Alphington for Australia Paper Manufacturing Ltd as a multi-storeyed glass box.

The 1956 Olympic Games kindled overseas interest in Melbourne and occasioned the new Olympic Swimming Pool, designed by Borland, McIntyre and J. and P. Murphy (now classified by the National Trust as an early example of pre-tensioned steel frame construction). The Myer Music Bowl appeared in 1959, a beautiful stressed skin structure designed by Yuncken, Freeman Bros, Griffiths and Simpson. Following the interest in the Sydney Opera House, Roy Grounds published his design for the Victorian National Gallery and Cultural Centre in 1961, a sombre jewel box with a face recalling the traditional solidarity of Malmsbury bluestone, and giving to Melbourne a landmark and centre for culture and the performing arts. This is still under construction.

In the 1960s the availability of metal deck revolutionized roof shapes and sharply-angled skillions appeared on exposed beams. This allowed clearstorey lighting and more exciting experiments in spatial comprehension. 'Cathedral' ceilings became fashionable over living areas and the Light Timber Framing Code alleviated the restrictions of the traditional framing regulations.

Further, the break away from the flat roof allowed the roof shape to be conceived as an energy exchanger. It could be orientated towards the sun at 38° to the horizontal to hold solar absorbers. The roof could also be used to deflect wind currents onto a

small windmill. The roofscape was no longer horizontal but expressed an energetic relationship to its surroundings.

After the war Melbourne still had a height limit set by the city by-laws and pressure to violate it was inevitable. John La Gerche introduced the curtain wall in aluminium at Gilbert Court, 100 Collins Street, in 1954. In 1956 Bates, Smart and McCutcheon produced the startlingly new I.C.I. House in East Melbourne, with its twenty storeys finishing at a height 175 per cent of the customary limit. This was the thin end, and since then many air-conditioned, glass-walled office towers have followed—Shell House (1958-60), National Mutual Centre (1962), Southern Cross Hotel (1962-63), etc. In the 1970s there was a dramatic increase in height, with buildings like B.H.P. House (1969-70), Nauru House (1976-77), Collins Place (begun 1970), Capital Tower (1977-79) and the State Bank Building (begun 1975).

In recent years there has been a growing concern about high energy consumption in air-conditioned buildings with insufficient insulation in their perimeter walls, and about the inevitable flow of commuter traffic to and from the city. Conservation of old buildings and historic areas, the creation of pedestrian precincts and the movement towards alternative energy lifestyles have become viable objectives. This has had an effect upon living patterns and home design, involving the re-use of old materials, and, in some cases, a return to mud bricks and grass roots.

With population growth slowing down, the suburban sprawl has temporarily halted, much to the chagrin of outer-area land developers, and the inner suburbs are being developed more intensively, as buildings which have outlived their original purposes are recycled into residential use. This is generally acknowledged to be a means of rejuvenation and of preserving the identity of an old area, and more desirable than the sterility resulting from wholesale demolition. Whereas high-rise Housing Commission flats arose from areas of rubble, today many local action groups are concerned about the identity of their own areas and the Commission's policy on urban renewal has changed away from demolition and towards small-scale housing and the preservation of old housing to preserve this identity.

A multi-racial, multi-cultural population is slowly becoming aware of the identity of Melbourne, the muddy village on the Yarra, the rip-roaring town of the gold rush days, the vigorous Victorian metropolis, the computerized high-rise city and recognizing its character. In *Melbourne on the Yarra* Marjorie Tipping concludes:

Melbourne, to me has few peers, if any, because I have always found the basic human ingredient of warmth emanating from the people of Melbourne irresistible. It makes most of us who have tried living elsewhere prefer to live here. It is a good and gracious place in which to live.

Notes

1   Explorers and Pioneers

1 Robert Douglass Boys, *First Years at Port Phillip 1834-1843*, Robertson and Mullens, Melbourne, 1959, pp.10, 11.

2 K.A. Austin, *The Voyage of the Investigator 1801-1803*, Rigby, Adelaide, 1964, p.131.

3 See, for instance, Francis P. Labilliere, *Early History of the Colony of Victoria*, Sampson Low, Marston, Searle and Rivington, London, 1878, vol.1.

4 James Bonwick, *Port Phillip Settlement*, Sampson Low, Marston, Searle and Rivington, London, 1883, p.80.

5 James Bonwick, *John Batman, the Founder of Victoria*, ed. C.E.Sayers, Wren Publishing, Melbourne, 1973, pp.24, 25, 84, 85.

6 E. Wilson Dobbs, *Rise and Growth of Architecture*, pamphlet produced by the *Australasian Builder and Contractors' News*, Sydney, 1892, p.10.

7 Robert Russell, 'Letters Home, Experiences in Port Phillip 1842-1847' *La Trobe Library Journal*, vol.2, no.6, October 1970, p.36.

8 J. Grant and G. Serle, *The Melbourne Scene 1803-1956*, Melbourne University Press, Melbourne, 1957, p.11.

9 Garryowen [Edmund Finn], *Chronicles of Early Melbourne 1835-1852*, Fergusson and Mitchell, Melbourne, 1888, pp.108, 109.

10 Notes and early letters in the care of the Brighton Historical Society by courtesy of the secretary, Mrs Rosalind Landells.

11 Alix Macdonald, 'The Doll's House', *Age*, Melbourne, 9 June 1972, p.15.

12 Professor Ernest Scott, *Dendy's Special Survey*, Victorian Historial Society Magazine, vol.x no.2, November 1924.

13 Weston A. Bate, *A History of Brighton*, Melbourne University Press, Melbourne, 1962, pp.48, 49.

14 John Butler Cooper, *The History of Prahran*, Modern Printing, Melbourne, 1924, p.28.

15 Denton Prout [pseud.] & Fred Feely, *50 Years Hard*, Rigby, Adelaide, 1967, p.64.

16 Wilson P.Evans, City of Williamstown Historian, historical notes on Williamstown.

2   Early Melbourne Architecture

1 Robert Russell, 'Letters home, Experiences in Port Phillip 1842-1847', *La Trobe Library Journal* vol.2, no.6, October 1970.

2 Miles B. Lewis, *Victorian Primitive*, Greenhouse Publications, Melbourne, 1977, p.64.

3 Readers are referred to Miles Lewis's book for a thorough treatment of this subject.

4 Robert D. Boys, *First Years at Port Phillip*, Robertson and Mullens, Melbourne, 1959, p.53.

5 Mark Twain, *More Tramps Abroad*, Chatto and Windus, London, 1897, p.107.

6 J.M. Freeland, *Architecture in Australia*, Cheshire, Melbourne, 1968, p.100.

7 B. Cook, *The Beginnings of Brunswick*, Victorian Historical Society Magazine, May 1921 vol.VIII no.2.

8 John Butler Cooper, *The History of Prahran*, Modern Printing, Melbourne, 1924, p.97.

9 From *Footscray's First Fifty Years*, published by the *Footscray Advertiser*, 1909. (Ed. E. Michell).

10 Miles B. Lewis, 'Architectural Drawings as Historical Sources', *La Trobe Library Journal*, vol.5, no.20, December 1977, p.80.

11 *Australian Encyclopaedia*, vol.5, p.288.

3 Melbourne after the Gold Rush

1 Geoffrey Serle, *The Golden Age*, Melbourne University Press, Melbourne, 1963, p.29.

2 Quoted by H.C.P. Turnbull, 'The Gold Rush, Desertion of Melbourne', *Argus*, Melbourne, 13 June 1931, p.5.

3 David Saunders, *Historic Buildings of Victoria*, Jacaranda in association with the National Trust, Melbourne, 1966, p.18.

4 Richard Twopeny, *Town Life in Australia*, Elliot Stock, London, 1883; Penguin Facsimile 1973, pp.31, 32.

5 *ibid.*, p.14.

6 Rev. S. Login, 'Reminiscences of Early Church Work in Victoria', *Southern Cross*, Melbourne, 20 November 1908, p.1110.

7 Niall Brennan, *The History of Nunawading*, Hawthorn Press, Melbourne, 1972, p.17.

8 *Australian Encyclopaedia*, vol.5, 'Houses and Housing'.

9 Michael Read, Prefabricated Buildings and Structures in the Colony of Victoria (Melbourne University Architectural School History IV Thesis).

10 Albert Mattingley, *The Early History of North Melbourne*, Victorian Historical Society Magazine, vol.5 no.3, 29 March 1917.

11 Edward Keep, *The Australian Ironmonger*, 1 November 1899, p.410.

12 Miles B. Lewis, article on prefabrication on Education page of *Trust Newsletter*, May 1971.

13 These are illustrated in *Early Melbourne Architecture 1840-1888* by Maie Casey and others, Oxford University Press, Melbourne, 1953, p.140.

14 Graeme E. Robertson quoting *The Illustrated London News* in *Victorian Heritage*, Georgian House, Melbourne, 1960, pp.45-8.

15 James Bonwick, *Western Victoria. The Narrative of an Edcational Tour in 1857*, Heinemann, Melbourne, 1970 (first published 1858), p.71.

16 J.M. Freeland, *The Making of a Profession*, Angus and Robertson, Sydney 1971, p.26.

17 Minutes of Victorian Institute of Architects, 5 April 1886, State Library of Victoria, La Trobe Collection.

18 Alexander Sutherland, *Victoria and its Metropolis*, McCarron, Bird and Co., Melbourne 1888, p.184.

19 *Argus*, 2 March 1859, quoted in Winston Burchett, *East Melbourne 1837-1977*, Craftsman Press, Melbourne, 1978, p.75.

20 Information from *See*, October 1978, *Argus*, 19 June 1857 and Colin Reilly of Brunswick.

21 Raymond Honey, review of *William Mason, the First New Zealand Architect* by John Stacpoole, *Journal of the Royal Institute of British Architects*, December 1972, p.516.

4 Gothic Revival

1 Robert Furneaux Jordan, *Victorian Architecture*, Penguin Books, 1966, Middlesex, U.K. p.79.

2 Colonel Percival Dale, *Melbourne's Churches and Cathedrals*, Victorian Historical Society Magazine, vol.33, no.2, November 1962.

3 John Betjeman, *A Pictorial History of English Architecture*, John Murray, London, 1970, p.33.

4 Kenneth Clark, *The Gothic Revival*, Penguin Books, 1964, Middlesex, U.K. p.155.

5 Preface to George Nadel, *Australia's Colonial Culture*, Melbourne, 1957, p.xi, quoted in Geoffrey Serle, *From Deserts and Prophets Come*, Heinemann, Melbourne, 1973, p.19.

6 J.M. Freeland, *Melbourne Churches 1836-1851*, Melbourne University Press, Melbourne, 1963, p.55.

7 *Australian Builder and Land Advertiser*, 5 February 1859, p.36.

8 Comment by a leading English art historian, quoted in Geoffrey Serle, *op.cit.*, p.47.

9 Morton Herman, *The Blackets, an Era of Australian Architecture*, Angus and Robertson, Sydney, 1963, p.91.

10 *ibid.*, p.187.

11 *ibid.*, p.186.

12 Nathaniel Billing's obituary quoted by Miles Lewis in 'Architectural Drawings as Historical Sources', *La Trobe Library Journal*, vol.5, no.20, December 1977.

13 Mary Turner Shaw, *Bates, Smart and McCutcheon Historical Survey, 1852-1972*, privately printed, p.1.

14 Alexander Sutherland, *Victoria and its Metropolis*, McCarron, Bird and Co., Melbourne, 1888 p.573.

15 John Summerson, *Heavenly Mansions*, Cresset Press, London, 1949, p.175.

16 Paul Thompson, *William Butterfield*, Routledge and Kegan Paul, London, 1971, pp.249, 250.

17 Minutes of Victorian Institute of Architects, 20 April 1891, State Library of Victoria, La Trobe Collection.

5 Late Victorian Melbourne

1 Richard Twopeny, *Town Life in Australia*, Elliot Stock, London, 1883; Penguin Facsimile 1973, pp.2, 3.

2 Quoted in W.H. Newnham, *Melbourne, the Biography of a City*, Cheshire, Melbourne, 1956, p.28.

3 Michael Cannon, *The Land Boomers*, Nelson, Melbourne, 1976, p.39.

4 Mark Twain, *More Tramps Abroad*, Chatto and Windus, London, 1887, pp.102, 103.

5 Geoffrey Serle, *The Golden Age*, Melbourne University Press, Melbourne, 1963, p.369.

6 Brian McKinlay, 'Marvellous Melbourne', *Educational Magazine*, vol.29, no.8, 1972.

7 'Victorian Representative Men at Home no.2, Sir Henry Wrixon', *Punch*, 27 August 1903, p.291.

8 *Australasian Builder and Contractors' News*, 16 August 1890, p.118.

9 *Sydney Daily Telegraph*, 27 February 1890, quoted in John D. Keating, *Mind the Curve*, Melbourne University Press, Melbourne, 1970, p.5.

10 Keating, *op.cit.*, p.74.

11 *Australasian Builder and Contractors' News*, 19 January 1889, p.69.

12 Cavity walls are shown in the contract drawings for a house at 17 St Vincent's Place, South Melbourne, designed in 1879 probably by Edward Twentyman. (Miles Lewis, 'Architectural Drawings as Historical Sources', *La Trobe Library Journal*, vol.5., no.20, December 1977.

13 Sally O'Neill in *Australian Dictionary of Biography*, vol.5, Melbourne University Press, Melbourne, 1974.

14 Alexander Sutherland, *Victoria and its Metropolis*, McCarron, Bird and Co., Melbourne, 1888, p.549.

15 Geoffrey Serle, *From Deserts the Prophets Come*, Heinemann, Melbourne, 1973, p.47.

16 *Australasian Builder and Contractors' News*, 30 June 1888, pp.425, 426.

17 Ken Edmonds, 'The Australia Building 'Skyscraper' 1889-1979?', *Architect*, December 1978, p.11.

18 For example, *Ornamental Cast Iron in Melbourne*, Georgian House, Melbourne, 1967; *Cast Iron Decoration: a World Survey*, Thames and Hudson, London, 1977, and *Parkville*, Georgian House, Melbourne, 1975. The latter two had Joan Robertson as co-author.

19 *Argus Weekend Magazine*, 17 May 1947, pp.16, 17.

20 *Trust Newsletter*, September 1973.

21 *Australasian Builder and Contractors' News*, 17 September 1887, p.302.

22 Geoffrey Serle, *From Deserts the Prophets Come*, p.1.

23 Lewis Mumford, *Sticks and Stones*, revised edition, Dover Publications, New York, 1955, p.136.

6 Federation Architecture

1 *Australasian Builder and Contractors' News*, 28 October 1893, p.216.

2 *The Illustrated Australian News*, 1 February 1894, p.22

3 David Saunders, 'Domestic Styles of Australia's Federation Period: Queen Anne and the Balcony Style', *Architecture in Australia, August 1969.*

4 *ibid.*

5 *ibid.*

6 *Real Property Annual*, no.7, August 1918, p.48.

7 *Real Property Annual*, no.6, August 1917, p.49.

8 Robin Boyd, *Australia's Home*, Penguin Books, Ringwood, 1968, p.71.

9 *Australasian Builder and Contractors' News*, 27 August 1892, p.105.

10 Geoffrey Woodfall, 'Harold Desbrowe Annear', *Architecture in Australia, February 1967.*

11 Verbal information from Wilson P. Evans, City of Williamstown Historian.

12 *Real Property Annual*, June 1913, p.68.

13 *Encyclopaedia of Victoria*, vol.2, p.48.

14 Royal Victorian Institute of Architects *Journal*, March 1910.

15 G.A.T. Middleton, *Modern Buildings, their Planning, Construction and Equipment*, Caxton Publishing, London 1906, pp.165, 166.

16 *Real Property Annual*, 1912, p.11.

7 Melbourne between the Wars

1 Quoted in ABC television documentary, 'Walter Burley Griffin, a Draftsman who went to Australia', 1971.

2 Donald Leslie Johnson, *The Architecture of Walter Burley Griffin*, Macmillan, Melbourne 1977, p.76.

3 Walter Burley Griffin, *Real Property Annual*, July 1921, p.36.

4 David Atwell, 'The Rise and Fall of the London Picture Palace', *Journal of the Royal Institute of British Architects,* January 1973.

5 *Australian Home Builder*, 15 November 1924, p.61.

6 Ray Tonkin, 'The AMP and Port Authority', *Architect*, journal of the Victorian Chapter of the R.A.I.A., September 1976.

7 J.M. Freeland, *The Making of a Profession*, Angus and Robertson, Sydney, 1971, p.281.

8 John Ruskin, *The Seven Lamps of Architecture*, George Allen, Orpington, Kent, 1886.

8 Melbourne as a Town Plan

1 David Saunders, *Look Here*, Cheshire, Melbourne, 1968, p.54.

2 Garryowen [Edmund Finn], *Chronicles of Early Melbourne 1835-1852*, Fergusson and Mitchell, Melbourne 1888.

3 Bernard Barrett, *The Inner Suburbs*, Melbourne University Press, Melbourne, 1971. This and other statements about Collingwood in this chapter come from this book.

4 J. Grant and G. Serle, *The Melbourne Scene 1803-1966*, Melbourne University Press, Melbourne, 1957, p.77.

5 Weston Bate, *A History of Brighton*, Melbourne University Press, Melbourne, 1962, p.36.

6 J.S. Gawler, *A Roof over my Head*, Lothian, Sydney, 1963, p.12.

7 John D. Keating, *Mind the Curve*, Melbourne University Press, Melbourne, 1970, p.56.

8 The theme of Melbourne's isolation is well described in Geoffrey Blainey, *The Tyranny of Distance*, Sun Books, Melbourne, 1966.

9 Graeme Davidson, *Public Utilities and the Expansion of Melbourne in the 1880s*, Australian Economic History Review, vol.X, no.2, September 1970, p.169.

10 Quoted by Lionel J. Skinner in notes prepared for the House Inspections Section of the National Trust of Australia (Victoria), 1972.

11 Asa Briggs, Victorian Cities, Pengiun Books, Middlesex, U.K., 1968, p.281.

12 *Plan of General Development. Melbourne. Report of Metropolitan Town Planning Commission 1929*, p.242.

Bibliography

General Background

SERLE, Geoffrey. *From Deserts the Prophets Come, The Creative Spirit in Australia 1788-1972*. Heinemann, Melbourne, 1973.

SERLE, Geoffrey. *The Golden Age, A History of the Colony of Victoria 1851-1861*. Melbourne University Press, Melbourne, 1963.

BOYS, Robert Douglass. *First Years at Port Phillip 1834-1842*. Robertson and Mullens, Melbourne, 1959.

BLAINEY, Geoffrey. *The Tyranny of Distance*. Sun Books, Melbourne, 1966.

NEWNHAM, W.H. *Melbourne, the Biography of a City*. Cheshire, Melbourne, 1956.

BELL, Agnes Paton. *Melbourne, John Batman's Village*. Cassell, Melbourne 1965.

CANNON, Michael. *The Land Boomers*. Melbourne University Press, Melbourne, 1966; Nelson, Melbourne, 1976.

BILLOTT, C.P. *John Batman and the Founding of Melbourne*. Hyland House, Melbourne, 1979.

GRANT, James & SERLE, Geoffrey. *The Melbourne Scene 1803-1956*. Melbourne University Press, Melbourne, 1957.

McGREGOR, Anne & SEDDON, George. *Somewhere to go on Sunday: A guide to Outdoor Melbourne*. Centre for Environmental Studies, University of Melbourne, 1978.

TIPPING, Marjorie. *Melbourne on the Yarra*. Lansdowne Editions, Melbourne, 1977.

DAVISON, Graeme. *The Rise and Fall of Marvellous Melbourne*. Melbourne University Press, Melbourne, 1979.

REED T.T. *Historic Churches of Australia* Macmillan, Melbourne, 1978.

DAVISON, Graeme. *The Rise and Fall of Marvellous Melbourne*, Melbourne University Press, Melbourne, 1979.

Regional Histories

BATE, Weston. *A History of Brighton*. Melbourne University Press, Melbourne, 1962.

BRENNAN, Niall, *The History of Nunawading*. Hawthorn Press, Melbourne 1972.

ROGERS, Dorothy. *A History of Kew*. Lowden Publishing, 1973.

COOPER, John Butler *The History of Prahran*. Modern Printing, Melbourne, 1924.

ROBERTSON E. Graeme & ROBERTSON, Joan. *Parkville*. Georgian House, Melbourne, 1975.

ROBERTSON, E. Graeme. *Carlton*. Rigby, 1974.

EVANS, Wilson P. *Port of Many Prows*. Hawthorn Press, Melbourne, 1969.

CUMMINS, Cyril (ed.). *Heidelberg since 1836, A Pictorial History*. Heidelberg Historical Society, Melbourne, 1971.

LEMON, Andrew. *Box Hill*. Lothian Publishing, Melbourne, 1978.

Architecture

FREELAND J.M. *Architecture in Australia*. Cheshire, Melbourne, 1968.

BOYD, Robin. *Australia's Home*, Melbourne University Press, Melbourne, 1952; Penguin Books, Ringwood, 1968.

CASEY, Maie and others. *Early Melbourne Architecture*. Oxford University Press, Melbourne, 1953.

LEWIS, Miles B. *Victorian Primitive*. Greenhouse Publications, Melbourne, 1977.

DAY, Norman. *Modern Houses Melbourne*. Brian Zouch Pubications, Melbourne, 1976.

ROBERTSON, E. Graeme. *Victorian Heritage*. Georgian House, Melbourne, 1960.

ROGAN, John P. *Melbourne* (National Trust Guide). Jacaranda, Brisbane, 1970.

Cox, Philip & Lucas, Clive. *Australian Colonial Architecture,* Lansdowne Editions, Melbourne, 1978.

Shaw, M.T. *Builders of Melbourne. The Cockrams and their Contemporaries 1853-1972.* Cypress Books, Melbourne 1972.

Australian Council Of National Trusts. *Historic Houses of Australia.* Cassell, Sydney, 1974.

Australian Council Of National Trusts. *Historic Public Buildings of Australia.* Cassell, Sydney, 1971.

Johnson, Donald Leslie. *The Architecture of Walter Burley Griffin.* Macmillan, Melbourne, 1977.

Freeland, J.M. *The Making of a Profession.* Angus and Robertson Melbourne 1971.

Glossary

adobe
Unburnt brick, dried in the sun, containing chopped straw. It was a traditional building material in semi-arid regions and many parts of Europe, and was naturally imported with the early settlers.

architrave
The lower 'layer' of a classical entablature. Generally, the moulded frame round a door or window opening.

balloon frame
Timber 'space-frame' construction, believed to have originated in America in the last century, incorporating bearers, joists, studs, plates and braces. More commonly known here as stud frame.

barge-board
A sloping board along a gable acting as a facia to the roofing timbers, sometimes elaborately decorated.

Baroque
The architecture of the seventeenth and early eighteenth centuries which expressed the ethos of the times in flowing wall surfaces, exuberant decoration and large-scale sweeping vistas.

bressumer
A horizontal beam on an external wall. In Queen Anne architecture this was often curved and decorative.

broach spire
A spire rising from a square tower without parapets. The broach is a triangular feature effecting the transition between the square tower and the octagonal spire.

campanile
A bell tower. In Italian Romanesque architecture this was a prominent and usually free-standing feature.

candle-snuffer roof
A non-technical term for a turret-like roof over a bay or ingle.

cartouche
A richly carved panel frequently found in Baroque architecture. Sometimes it bears an inscription and crowns a broken pediment.

cesspit
A pit for the collection of sewage before the days of modern sewage disposal.

clinker
An over-burnt brick presenting a rough dark-bluish impervious face.

couple
Framing rafters forming a pitched roof without ceiling ties.

coursed random rubble
Rough unhewn building stones with wide joints, and laid with deep courses.

cradle roof
Sometimes referred to as wagon roof. A roof with a series of arched braces supporting purlins and rafters.

damp-proof course
A horizontal layer of impervious material, in this context, usually slate, laid in a mortar joint, to prevent the passage of moisture rising up a wall.

dressings
Hewn masonry or better-quality brickwork used up the jambs of openings or the quoin (French for corner) of a wall.

English bond
A brick bond in which a course entirely of stretchers alternates with a course entirely of headers.

finial
The tip of a gable or pinnacle. It could be of decorative metalwork, carved stonework or moulded terra cotta.

firebrick
Brick made with a high content of quartz to withstand high temperatures.

flutings
Vertical concave mouldings round a column.

footing
The base structure of a wall widened out to distribute the load on to the foundations.

horizontal slab
Primitive wall construction of split timber laid horizontally between uprights. The uprights were set into the ground, and usually grooved to take the 'slabs' (timbers).

177

ingle or inglenook
A bay or recess off the main living area enclosing the fireplace, usually with seats on either side of it.

keystone
The centre stone in an arch.

lathing
A base for plaster, in this context sawn or split strips of wood 1 to 1¼ inches by ¼ to ½ inch fixed with gaps between them.

lintol (or lintel)
A horizontal structural member bridging an opening.

moulding
The contours given to projecting members, designed to give certain shadow effects.

mullion
An upright post in a window frame which serves to divide the opening or fixed lights.

nave, choir, transepts
Components in the traditional 'western' church or cathedral plan.

niche
A semi-circular recess in a wall surmounted by a semi-dome, often used as a setting for an urn or statue.

orders of architecture
A system of column and entablature according to a discipline of proportion and detail defined by Vitruvius and later by Serlio. There were three Greek orders: Doric, Ionic and Corinthian, and the Romans added two more, Tuscan and Composite. There was also the Roman Doric.

Palladian
According to the principles and publications of Palladio (1508-80), the most influential of the Italian architects. Palladianism under Lord Burlington's patronage was the dominating force in the architecture of the eighteenth century in England.

pendentive
The transition between a square compartment and a circular dome, used for the first time in Byzantine architecture. It consists of a concave spandrel leading from the angle of the two walls to the base of the circular dome.

pilaster
A shallow pier or rectangular column projecting from a wall, and, in classical architecture, conforming to and 'echoing' a column from one of the orders.

pinnacle
A steep termination at the top of a spire or buttress or angle of a parapet, sometimes decorated with crockets.

porte-cochère
A porch large enough for wheeled vehicles to pass through.

purlin
A horizontal member in roof framing running parallel with the ridge and providing support for the rafters.

quartering
Sawn timber cut as nearly as possible radially, with no growth ring at an angle of less than 80° to the surface.

quatrefoil
A circular shape in tracery incorporating cusping like a four-leaved clover.

Regency
The style current under the Prince Regent (George IV) in the 1820s, and, more generally, in the early part of the nineteenth century.

scantlings
In this context sawn timber for roof framing.

Romanesque
The style current in Europe from the eighth century until the coming of Gothic.

shingles
Wooden tiles of split hardwood for covering roofs. They were sometimes of cedar.

string course
A continuous projecting horizontal band set in the surface of a wall and usually moulded.

stucco
Smooth plastering to the outside of a wall.

tetrastyle portico
A portico in the classical style with four columns.

tracery
Ornamental piercing in the stonework
filling the upper part of a Gothic window.
The patterns so formed usually
incorporated little curves called cusping.

tuck pointing
Pointing where the joints are first filled
flush and then grooved to form a 'tuck'.
White lime putty in the tuck emphasized
the joint.

List of Architects

The following architects are referred to in the text.

name	in practice	partners and other details
AALTO Alvar 1898-1976		Finnish architect whose influence was felt in the Modern Movement through the use of natural materials and through such innovative buildings as the Convalescent Home at Paimio (1929-33).
ADDISON George Henry Male	1885-99	Oakden, Addison and Kemp.
ALSOP Rodney Howard 1881-1932		Klingender and Alsop 1900-04. He also worked with Bramwell Smith in a short term partnership and with Conrad Sayce on the Winthrop Hall competition. He was the first Director of the University of Melbourne Architectural Atelier.
ANNEAR Harold Desbrowe 1866-1933		An Australian-born architect known for much innovative work in the field of house design and in the movement towards an indigenous Australian style.
ANTHONESS T.	1889-94	No partners listed. Chiefly hotel work such as the Old Royal Hotel, Nelson Place, Williamstown.
ASHWORTH Thomas Ramsden 1864-1935		Fawcett and Ashworth. Winner of the competition for Flinders Street Station. Associated with Desbrowe Annear in the design for the Church Street Bridge
ASKEW David Christopher 1854-1906		Born in Cumberland, emigrated 1869. Twentyman and Askew 1883-1906 (Askew was Twentyman's brother-in-law). Warehouses, shops, offices.
AUSTIN G.H.B. 1859-1921		Architect in Department of Public Works.
BALLANTYNE Cedric Heise 1875-1957		Ballantyne C.H. and Associates; Ballantyne and Hare; Ballantyne and Sneddon; Oakden and Ballantyne; Oakden, Ballantyne and Hare.
BARLOW Marcus R. 1890-1955	1892-1950	Grainger and Barlow 1914-18; Grainger, Little and Barlow 1918-20 (several partnerships). Factories, houses. A well-known Melbourne architect whose son has carried on the practice now know as Marcus Barlow and Associates.

BARNES Frederick d.1884	1862-83	Reed and Barnes 1862-83. Worked with Joseph Reed, was a fine draughtsman and designed many of Melbourne's buildings during this period.
BARNET Nahum 1855-1931	1879-1931	Commercial work, houses, factories.
BARRETT Charles	1886-89	Designed Holy Trinity Church, Kew.
BARRY Sir Charles 1795-1860		An early Victorian architect who designed the Reform Club in London and, with Pugin, the Houses of Parliament (1839-52).
BARTLETT Harold E. b.1902		Leith and Bartlett 1936-.
BASTOW Henry R.	1911-42	No partners listed.
BATES Edward Albert 1865-1931	1889-1931	Hyndman and Bates 1892-1900; Bates, Peebles and Smart; Bates, Smart and McCutcheon.
BAUDOT Anatole de 1834-1915		A French architect influential in the development of reinforced concrete.
BEASLEY Hillson	1886-96	Beasley and Little 1895-96.
BEAVER Isidor G. d.1934	1892-1934	Born in Manchester, emigrated to Adelaide, then practised in Melbourne for about forty-five years. Wright and Beaver 1892; Wright, Reed and Beaver 1893; Beaver and Purnell 1918-34.
BILLING Nathaniel 1821-1910		An English-trained architect of the Gothic Revival who settled first at Belfast (Port Fairy) and did commercial work, houses and churches throughout Victoria.
BILLSON Edward Fielder b.1892	1931-	Billson and Mewton, E.F. Billson and Associates. Worked with Walter Burley Griffin and won the competition for the University of Auckland. Houses and flats. Firm is currently E.F. Billson and Associates.
BLACKBURN James (snr) 1803-54		Transported to Hobart for forgery and eventually became Melbourne City Surveyor. His best known achievement was the Yan Yean water scheme (1854).

BLACKBURN James (jnr)	1864-78	Newson and Blackburn. Responsible for houses, hotels, commercial work and churches, including St Mark's, Fitzroy, and St Stephen's, Richmond.
BLACKETT Cyril 1857-1937		Son of Edmund (see below).
BLACKETT Edmund T 1818-83		English-born Gothic Revival architect most of whose work is to be found in New South Wales. Designed the Clarte Buildings at Trinity College, University of Melbourne (1883).
BLACKET William Arthur Mordey 1874-1962		Blacket and Forster; Blacket and Rankin; Blacket, Forster and Craig. Amongst other things in a varied practice he designed the Presbyterian church in Heidelberg.
BORLAND Kevin b.1926		Borland, McIntyre, J and P. Murphey. Now Professor of Architecture at Deakin University.
BOYD Robin Gerard Penleigh 1919-71		Grounds, Romberg and Boyd. Innovative designer, well known for some outstanding houses, and author of several architectural works.
BREUER Marcel b.1902		Hungarian-born architect prominent in the Modern Movement in Germany and U.S.A.
BROWNE George b.1813		Houses, commercial work, religious buildings.
BRUNELLESCHI Filippo 1377-1446		An early Renaissance architect most of whose work is to be seen in Florence. Renowned for the dome of Florence Cathedral and for the Pazzi Chapel.
BUCHAN Tom Johnstone 1876-1962	1914-	Laird and Buchan, Geelong and Colac 1914-36. Buchan, Laird and Buchan 1936-. Extensive work in the Western District of Victoria.
BUCHAN Sir John, son of T.J. Buchan b.1909-	1936-	Buchan, Laird and Buchan, now in practice in Melbourne as well as Geelong.

BULL Frederick William	1859-75	A Collingwood carpenter, Borough Architect of Williamstown, designed Mandalay, 24 The Strand, Williamstown (1852).
BUTLER Charles	1920-	Well-known architect and designer of many large houses in Melbourne.
BUTLER Walter Richmond 1864-1949		Butler and Ussher; Inskip and Butler; Butler W.R. and Martin; Butler W. and R.; Butler W. and R. and Pettit. Houses and churches.
BUTTERFIELD William 1814-1900		An English architect of the Gothic Revival who designed St Peter's Cathedral, Adelaide, and St Paul's Cathedral, Melbourne.
CALDER Stuart P. b.1893	1961-	A Melbourne architect.
CARLETON A.E.H. d.1936		Ward and Carleton 1899-1900; Carleton and Carleton.
CHEETHAM F. Keith	1925-33	No partners listed.
CHERMAYEFF Serge b.1900		An architect prominent in the European Modern Movement in the 1930s. Practised in London.
CLARK Edward James b.1868	1912-21	Son of J.J. Clark (see below).
CLARK John James 1838-1915		J.J. and E.J. Clark 1912-21. A Melbourne architect in public service who also practised in Brisbane. Assumed to have designed the Treasury Building in 1857.
COATES Wells 1895-1958		An English architect prominent in the Modern Movement of the 1930s.
COWPER Christopher A. b.1868	1892-1945	A Melbourne architect born in Cape Town, commenced practice in his own name in 1891. Cowper, Murphy and Appleford 1926-1945.
CRAWFORD H.R.	1908-33	A Melbourne architect.

CROUCH Thomas James 1832-89		Born in Tasmania, Mayor of St Kilda. Crouch and Wilson. Churches, banks, public buildings, houses.
D'EBRO Charles A 1849 (or 50)-1920		D'Ebro, MacKenzie and Meldrum; D'Ebro and Meldrum; D'Ebro, Meldrum and Wagstaff. A London-trained architect who did commercial work and houses, including Stonnington in Malvern (1892).
DENNEHY R.J.	1883-91	Tappin, Dennehy and Gilbert 1886-91.
DOBBS E. Wilson	1893-1905	No partners listed.
DODS Robin S. b.1920		Hall and Dods 1949-. Also practised in Sydney and Brisbane.
DOWDEN R.A.	1858-61	Dowden and Ross. Houses, churches, schools. A pupil of John Gill.
DUGUID A.E.	1886-98	Houses, churches, commercial work.
DUNN Alfred 1865-94		Tayler and Dunn. Amongst other things this partnership designed the C.B.A. Head Office, 335 Collins Street (1891).
EBERSON John 1875 (?)-1954		A New York architect mentioned in the design of the State Theatre (Forum).
EGGLESTON Alec Stanley 1883-1955		A.S. Eggleston 1905-12; Eggleston and Oakley 1912-; Eggleston A.S. and R.A. 1937-; Eggleston, MacDonald and Secomb 1954-. R.V.I.A. Bronze Medallist and author of *The Practising Architect*.
ELLERKER William Henry d.1891	1859-91	Ellerker and Kilburn 1886-1890. Ellerker and Co.
EVANS George de Lacy 1863-1937	1888-1937	Melbourne first, then Longwarry in Gippsland 1920-1937. Commercial work.
EVERETT Percy Edgar	1920-31	Chief Architect of the Public Works Department. Seeley, King and Everett.
FAWCETT James d.1934	1895-1934	Fawcett and Ashworth. Chief Architect of the Victorian Railways Department.

FILDES Alan L.   1936-   Seabrook and Fildes.
b.1921

FISHER   1891-1921   Fisher and Backhouse 1921. Houses, fire stations, churches.
Arthur H.

FITTS   Tayler, Lloyd and Fitts.
Frederick A.
d.1902

FOX James   1880-1900   Terry, Oakden and Fox 1880-1884; Fox and Oakden 1884-1900. Work extended to
Henry   Geelong, Hamilton and Ballarat.
d.1900

FRY Edwin   English architect of the Modern Movement of the 1930s. Houses, flats, industrial
Maxwell   design. Author of 'Fine Building'.
b.1899

FREEMAN   Yuncken, Freeman and Freeman; Yuncken, Freeman Bros. Griffiths and Simpson.
John R.   Yuncken Freeman Pty Ltd.
1899-1964

GAUDI Antoni   A highly eclectic architect who practised at Barcelona in a style influenced by
1852-1926   Gothic and Moorish elements.

GEORGE James 1858-   George and Schneider 1858-. Commercial work, churches.

GILBERT   1884-1914   Tappin, Gilbert and Dennehy in Melbourne. 1914, Healesville, no partner.
Charles N.

GILL John   1853-66   First listed in 1853 but may have been in practice some years earlier. Office at 55
c.1797-1866   Spring Street 1853-66. One of the pioneer architects in Victoria.

GODFREY   Godfrey and Spowers; Godfrey, Spowers, Hughes, Mewton and Lobb.
William Purves
Race
b.1907

GOODHUE   An American architect two developed his own style of freelance Gothic
Bertram   reminiscient of Perpendicular.
1869-1924

GRAINGER John H. d.1920		Father of Percy Grainger. Grainger and D'Ebro 1884-; Grainger, Kennedy and Little; Grainger and Little 1918-20; Grainger, Little and Barlow; Grainger, Little, Barlow and Hawkins; Grainger and Naish; Chief Architect of Public Works in Western Australia.
GRANT Leslie Gordon 1905-78	1961-	A Melbourne architect who worked with Walter Burley Griffin.
GREEN Frederick G	1890-95	A Melbourne architect.
GREENWAY Francis 1777-1837		An architect from Bristol deported to New South Wales for forgery. Employed by Governor Macquarie and stamped his image upon the early architecture of New South Wales. Many buildings designed by him still stand and are in use.
GREY Frederick William	1890-1898	Lawson and Grey
GRIFFIN Walter Burley 1876-1937		An American-born architect who came to Australia as a result of winning the Canberra competition in 1911.
GRIFFITHS William Balcombe b.1907	1938-77	Yuncken, Freeman and Griffiths 1938-62. Retired 1977.
GROPIUS Walter 1883-1969		A German-born architect whose Bauhaus movement had an untold influence on modern design of the 1930s. He migrated to England and then to U.S.A.
GROUNDS Sir Roy b.1905		Mewton and Grounds; Grounds, Romberg and Boyd; Grounds and Romberg. An architect responsible for many houses and flats. His greatest work is the Victorian Arts Centre.
HADDON Robert Joseph 1866-1929		Houses, churches. Leading academic and educationalist of the Edwardian period. Responsible for elevations and perspectives for other architects. Chief lecturer in architecture at the Working Men's College (now the Royal Melbourne Institute of Technology).

HAMILTON Robert Bell b.1892	1920s and 30s	Hamilton and Norris. Houses, especially of the pseudo-Tudor variety in Toorak.
HARE Henry	1923-33	Hare and Ballantyne 1923-25; Oakden, Ballantyne and Hare 1925-26. Hare and Hare 1926-29; Hare, Peck and Lacey 1930-33.
HAWKINS George Frederick	1920s and 30s	Barlow and Hawkins. Left the firm in 1932 to go to Western Australia.
HENDERSON Anketell Matthew 1853-1922		A. and K. Henderson; Henderson, Alsop and Martin; Reed, Henderson and Smart; Henderson and Smart.
HENDERSON Kingsley Anketell d.1942		Son of A.M. Henderson. The above partnerships were responsible for much commercial work, especially banks and much of Collins Street. Outside the profession he was the brains behind the *Argus* and 3XY.
HOLLINSHED Charles Neville	1929-65	A Melbourne architect.
HOOD Raymond 1881-1934		A New York architect.
HOPKINS Rhys E. b.1910	1936-	Hopkins and Van Rompaey 1960-; Rhys E. Hopkins.
HORTA Baron Victor 1861-1947		A Belgian architect and leading figure in the Art Nouveau movement.
HUDSON Philip Burgoyne	1910-40	Hudson, Wardrop and Ussher. Hudson, Wardrop 1921-.
HUNT Horbury 1838-1904		An architect of New South Wales who built many churches. His only known work in Melbourne is 38 Black Street, Brighton.
HYNDMAN R. Gordon d.1901	1890-1900	Hyndman and Bates 1892-1900.
INSKIP George Charles	1887-92	Inskip and Robertson 1890-92.

IRWIN Leighton
Francis 1892-1962

Irwin and Stephenson; Leighton Irwin and Co. Pty Ltd; Hospitals. Director of the University of Melbourne Architectural Atelier for twenty years.

JACKSON
Samuel
1807-76

Melbourne's first architect and builder, who came from Van Diemen's Land with Fawkner's party in 1835. He died at Enfield near London.

JOBBINS
George
1842-1921

1887-1921

Commercial and public buildings in Melbourne.

JOHNSON
Arthur Ebden
1821-95

Smith and Johnson. Commercial work, houses, public buildings, including the General Post Office and Law Courts.

JOHNSON
Harry M.G.

A Sydney architect.

JONES George
Sydney
1865-1927

A Sydney architect.

KEMP Henry
Hardie
1859-1946

1888-1940

Addison and Kemp 1888-89; Addison, Kemp and Oakden 1890-99; Kemp and Ussher 1900-06; Inskip and Kemp 1907-14; H.H. Kemp and F.B. Kemp 1928-40.

KEMP Thomas
1819-85

Knight, Kemp and Kerr. Returned to England in 1855.

KEMTER
George Alfred

1920-39

Peck and Kemter 1920-38; Peck, Kemter and Dalton 1939.

KERR Peter
1820-1912

Knight, Kemp and Kerr; Knight and Kerr. A Scottish-born architect who had worked for Charles Barry and was subsequently responsible for some of Melbourne's public buildings.

KILBURN
Edward George
1859-94

Ellerker, Kilburn and Pitt; Ellerker and Kilburn 1886-90.

KIRKPATRICK
R.A.

1889-94

Kirkpatrick and Giles 1890-91. Also practised in Sydney.

KLINGENDER Frederick Louis	1889-1939	Klingender and Alsop 1900-04; Klingender and Newbegin 1905-22. Klingender and Hamilton 1923-26; F.L. and K. Klingender 1927-39; President of R.V.I.A. 1935-37.
KNIGHT John George 1824-92		Knight, Kemp and Kerr; Knight and Kerr. A London-born architect prominent in the architectural profession in Melbourne.
LA GERCHE John A. b.1914	1955-	A Melbourne architect.
LAING Charles 1809 (?)-57		An architect who practised in Manchester and became Melbourne City Surveyor. Won the competition for Princes Bridge (1844) and designed the tower for St James's Old Cathedral (1840s).
LAIRD Ewan Campbell b.1907		Laird and Buchan 1914-36, Geelong and Colac. Buchan, Laird and Buchan, 1936-, Geelong and Melbourne.
LAWSON R.A.	1892-98	Lawson and Grey.
LE CORBUSIER (Charles-Edouard Jeanneret) 1887-1966		The most outstanding European architect of the Modern Movement.
LEITH A.C. 1897-1972		A.C. Leith and Associates 1927-36; Leith and Bartlett 1936- (previously the firm was known as George Brown Leith).
LIPPINCOTT Roy Alstan 1885-1969		An American architect, brother-in-law and partner of Walter Burley Griffin.
LOVE Allan Rhynhart 1909-80	1936-	Scarborough, Robertson and Love 1936-1940. (Scarborough and Associates 1940-).
MACKINTOSH Charles Rennie 1868-1928		A Scottish architect and exponent of Art Nouveau. Famous for the School of Art Building in Glasgow.
MCCUTCHEON Sir Osborn b.1899	1926-	Bates, Smart and McCutcheon, a continuation of the firm begun by Joseph Reed in 1884 after the death of Frederick Barnes.

McGRATH Raymond	1920-	Won scholarship in Sydney for training in London. Now in practice in London.
McINTYRE Peter b.1927	1961-	Borland, McIntyre, J. and P. Murphy; McIntyre, McIntyre and Partners Pty Ltd.
McIVER Evander 1834-1902		Employed by the Shire of Broadmeadows for 39 years. He built 22 Presbyterian churches in Victoria and was influenced by the American Romanesque style.
McMULLEN George	1888-92	Houses, commercial work.
MARSH Robert	1936-69	Marsh and Michaelson 1936-52.
MELDRUM Percy H. 1887-1968		Meldrum and Noad; Stephenson and Meldrum. Meldrum and Partners.
MENDELSOHN Eric 1887-1953		A German architect of the Modern Movement who introduced streamlined and curvaceous shapes in concrete.
MERRETT Samuel Hendon d.1883		He and his brother Thomas Henry are credited with the design and construction of the Crystal Palace for the Melbourne Exhibition of 1854.
MEWTON Geoffrey b.1905		Mewton and Grounds. Significant work in Melbourne, especially in the 1930s.
MICHAELSON F.	1936-65	Marsh and Michaelson 1936-52, now Marsh and Benny.
MOHOLY-NAGY Laszlo 1895-1946	1920-	European architect and photographer.
MURPHY J. AND P. b.1920 and 1924		Borland, McIntyre and J. and P. Murphy.
NASH John 1752-1835		A London architect and town planner who enjoyed the patronage of the Prince Regent.
NESFIELD Eden 1835-1888		Architect in partnership with Norman Shaw.

190

NEWSON Arthur	1849-	Newson and Blackburn, designed 'Bishopscourt' in 1849, also St Stephen's, Richmond, and St Mark's, Fitzroy.
NICHOLLS Eric	1925-41	In partnership with Walter Burley Griffin and later practised on his own.
NORRIS Harry N 1887-1966		A Melbourne architect.
NORTH Alexander 1859-1945		Corrie and North, North and Williams.
OAKDEN Percy 1845-1917		Terry and Oakden; Oakden, Addison and Kemp; Oakden and Kemp; Oakden and Ballantyne. A Tasmanian architect trained in London. Work is characterized by multi-coloured brickwork. Churches and institutional work. Designed Building I of the Royal Melbourne Institute of Technology.
OAKLEY Percy Allport 1883-1955		Oakley and Parkes 1930-. President of R.V.I.A. 1926-28.
OGG Charles A. d.1932	1902-32	Smith, Serpell and Ogg 1921-32.
OVEREND Acheson Best b. 1909	1934-	H. Vivian Taylor, Soillieux and Overend 1934-1939. Best Overend 1939-.
PARKES Stanley T. b.1894	1926-	Oakley and Parkes 1930-. Chairman of Architects' Registration Board for many years. Active in Legacy.
PECK Hugh Leonard	1920-39	Peck and Kemter, in association with Walter Burley Griffin on the Capitol Theatre. Peck, Kemter and Dalton 1939.
PITT William 1855-1918		Pitt and Walkley. Ellerker, Kilburn and Pitt. An Australian-trained architect whose work epitomizes the Melbourne Boom style of the 1880s.
PLAISTED Arthur W. 1890(?)-1965	1915-50	Plaisted and Warner 1932-50.
PLOTTEL Joseph 1883-1965	1911-65	A Melbourne architect responsible for the Footscray Town Hall and Beehive Building in Elizabeth Street.

POWER Joseph P.	1899-	Sulman and Power 1899. Also in Sydney.
PURCHAS Major Albert d.1909	1857-1909	Purchas and Swyer 1857-61. Houses, commercial work, funerary buildings and churches such as Christ Church and St George's, St Kilda, and the Presbyterian, East St Kilda.
PURCHAS Guyon	1885-1919	Son of above. Purchas and Teague 1902-20. Purchas and Shieleds 1903.
PURNELL Arthur William	1912-62	Purnell and Pearce 1937-62. Purnell and Beaver 1921-32.
RAHT Edward E.		Architect of New York, Sydney and Melbourne.
REED Joseph 1828-90		Reed and Barnes 1862-83. Reed, Henderson and Smart 1883-90. Wright, Reed and Beaver. Reed, Smart and Tappin 1890-1907. A Cornishman who dominated the architectural profession in Melbourne. First president of the second Victorian Institute of Architects 1871-74.
REYNOLDS Dunstan B.	1923-37	Craig, Reynolds and Garrett 1931-37.
RICHARDSON H.H. 1838-86		American architect whose work shows the strong influence of French Romanesque.
ROBERTSON J. Kirkland b.1909	1936-40	Scarborough, Robertson and Love 1936-40.
ROMBERG Professor Frederick b.1913		Grounds, Romberg and Boyd. An academic and practising architect whose innovative work can be seen in such buildings as Newburn Flats, Queens Road, South Melbourne.
ROSS David	1858-61	Dowden and Ross.
RUSSELL Robert 1807-1900		Russell and Watts; Russell, Watts and Pritchard. Worked in England for John Nash and became surveyor of early Melbourne. Architect and artist.
SALWAY William d.1903		Commercial work, public buildings, houses.

SAYCE Conrad c.1888	1925-27	Alsop and Sayce.
SCARBOROUGH John F. Deighton c.1899-c.1976	1934-	Scarborough, Robertson and Love 1936-40.
SCHNEIDER Joseph A.	1858-	James George and Joseph Schneider.
SEABROOK Norman Hugh	1936-	Seabrook and Fildes.
SEIDLER Harry b.1923	1948-	Sydney architect prominent in the Modern Movement.
SERPELL Charles Edward 1880-1962		Smith, Ogg and Serpell 1921-32.
SHAW Mary Turner b.1906	1932-68	Romberg and Shaw 1940-42. Architect and historian. Author of *Builders of Melbourne.*
SHAW Richard Norman 1831-1912		English architect generally regarded as the creator of the Queen Anne style.
SHIELDS William McMichael	1903-42	Purchas and Shields 1903-.
SIMPSON R. McC.	1939-62	Yuncken, Freeman Bros. Griffiths and Simpson.
SMART Francis Joseph 1852-1907		Henderson and Smart; Reed, Henderson and Smart 1883-90; Reed, Smart and Tappin 1890-1907; Tappin, Dennehy and Smart; Smart, Tappin and Peebles 1907.
SMITH Alfred Louis d.1907	1859-1906	Smith and Johnson 1880-1906. Smith and Pritchard.

SMITH A. Bramwell 1898-1975		Alsop and Smith, 1930-33. Also in Department of Works.
SMITH Sydney W. (snr) d.1886		Smith and Ogg.
SMITH Sydney (jnr) 1868-1933		Smith, Ogg and Serpell.
SOILLIEUX G.A. 1888-1967	1926-40	Taylor H., Vivian and Soillieux; H. Vivian Taylor, Soillieux and Overend 1936-40. A member of the assessment panel for the U.N. Secretariat Building, New York.
SPEIGHT Richard d.1901	1889-98	Speight and D'Ebro.
SPOWERS Henry Howard		Godfrey and Spowers; Godfrey, Spowers, Hughes, Mewton and Lobb.
STAPLEY Frank 1858-1918		Commercial work, houses. Lord Mayor of Melbourne.
STEPHENSON Sir Arthur 1890-1967		Stephenson and Meldrum; Stephenson and Turner. A Melbourne architect prominent in the field of hospital design. Awarded Royal Gold Medal 1954.
SULLIVAN Louis Henry 1856-1924		American architect influential in the 'Chicago' school.
SULMAN Sir John 1849-1934	1872-1934	In practice in Sydney. Sulman and Blackmann 1876. Sulman and Power 1899. Designed building for A.M.P., cr Collins and William Streets 1876. Sulman and Vernon 1900. Lecturer at Sydney University. Instituted Sulman Prize 1934.
SWYER Charles R.	1857-61	Purchas and Swyer.
TAPPIN William Britain 1854-1905		Reed, Smart and Tappin 1890-1907; Tappin, Gilbert and Dennehy 1886-1891. Born under canvas at Ballarat. His life was marked by 'gentleness and probity'.

TAYLER Lloyd 1830-1900		Tayler and Fitts 1893-1900; Tayler and Dunn; Vissieux and Tayler. One of the best-known architects of the day who lived in Brighton. Designed the C.B.A. Head Office, 335 Collins Street, and the Metropolitan Fire Brigade at Eastern Hill.
TAYLOR H. Vivian b.1894	1940-	Taylor and Soillieux 1923-36; H. Vivian Taylor, Soillieux and Overend 1936-40.
TEAGUE George Eric		Purchas and Teague 1902-20.
TERRY Leonard 1825-84		Terry and Oakden. Born in Yorkshire and became Diocesan Architect in Victoria. Supervising architect for St Paul's Cathedral. A competent, highly sensitive designer.
TOMPKINS H.W. c.1859-c.1953	1904	H.W. and F.B. Tompkins. Responsible for Commercial Travellers' Association Building in Flinders Street (1894), and for the new C.T.A. (1913), one of the first steel-framed buildings in Melbourne. Architects for Myer Emporium and Herald and Weekly Times.
TOMPKINS F.B. c.1861-c.1939		see above
TREEBY Philip Edward b.1860	1886-93	A Melbourne architect.
TURNER D.K.		Stephenson and Turner.
TWENTYMAN Edward		Twentyman and Askew. An architect from Cumberland who designed warehouses and the Block Arcade.
USSHER Beverley 1868-1908		Butler and Ussher; Ussher and Kemp. Chiefly Queen Anne Houses.
VELDE Henry van der 1863-1957		A Belgian architect who was influential in the Art Nouveau movement.
VERNON W.L.		Wardell and Vernon in Sydney 1884-99. Sulman and Vernon 1900-.

VICKERS Charles		Wharton and Vickers, commercial work and religious buildings.
VOYSEY Charles F. Annersley 1857-1941		English architect famous for his country houses.
WALKLEY Albion H. 1882-1968		Pitt and Walkley. Continued after Pitt's death in 1918.
WARDELL William Wilkinson 1823-99		Wardell and Vernon. Born in London, he designed thirty churches in England between 1846 and 1858. He became Inspector-General of Public Works and designed churches all over Victoria. He completed his career in Sydney.
WARDROP James Hastie 1891-1975		Hudson and Wardrop.
WARNER Laurence b.1904	1932-	Plaisted and Warner 1932-50.
WATTS Thomas 1827-1915		Russell and Watts; Russell, Watts and Pritchard; Smith and Watts; Thomas Watts and Son. Born in Gloucestershire. Designed West Melbourne Presbyterian Church and Sands and McDougall's factory.
WEBB Charles 1821-98		Webb, Charles and Sons. Webb, James and Charles. Webb and Taylor. Born in Suffolk, he was 'the first really sophisticated architect to appear in Melbourne'. (Lewis).
WEBB James 1808-70		Migrated to Victoria before Charles. Their partnership produced many churches and houses, especially in the Brighton area.
WEBB Philip 1831-1915		An English architect who designed 'Red House' in Bexley Heath for William Morris (1859).
WELLS William Elliot	1882-1908	Wells, William E. and Son.

WHITE Francis
Maloney
1819-88 White, F.M. and Son. Commercial work. The firm carried on under his son Alfred till 1901.

WHITE Henry E. 1922-27 White and Gurney 1922-27.

WILKINSON 1894-1906 Wilkinson and Permewan 1894.
John

WILKINSON
Prof. Leslie H.
1882-1973 A Sydney architect generally regarded as responsible for introducing the Spanish Mission style to Australia.

WILLIAMS
Louis Reginald
1890-1980 Born in Hobart. North and Williams; Williams and Cockrell. Churches in his own free interpretation of Gothic.

WILSON
W. Hardy
1881-1955 A New South Wales architect.

WILSON Ralph 1876-87 Beswicke and Wilson 1880-83; Crouch and Wilson 1884-87. Designed churches and
b.1827 the Malvern Town Hall.

WREN Sir
Christopher
1632-1723 An English architect whose achievement in the Renaissance is unsurpassed. London is rich with his work.

WRIGHT Frank
Lloyd 1869-1959 A great American architect who had a powerful effect on the course of the Modern Movement.

WRIGHT 1892-1917 Wright, Reed and Beaver. Came from Adelaide with Beaver.
Edmund William

YUNCKEN Otto
Abrecht 1903-51 Yuncken, Freeman and Freeman; Yuncken, Freeman Bros, Griffiths and Simpson; Yuncken Freeman Pty Ltd. Awarded Royal Humane Society Gold Medal.

References

Australian Dictionary of Biography, Melbourne University Press, Melbourne, 1966-.

The Cyclopedia of Victoria, vol.1, 'Architects', Melbourne, 1903.

John Fleming, Hugh Honour & Nikolaus Pevsner, The Penguin Dictionary of Architecture, Penguin Books, Middlesex, U.K. 1966.

Miles Lewis, Architectural Survey, National Estate Project 244, Urban Conservation Working Papers no. 24, Department of Architecture and Building, University of Melbourne 1977.

Miles Lewis, Notes on Architects represented in Exhibition of Architectural Drawings in La Trobe Library 1975.

Errol G. Knox, Who's Who in Australia, Herald Press, Melbourne, 1933-.

Journals of the Royal Victorian Institute of Architects.

Index

200